Dominating Dominia

A Type II Tournament Player's Guide for
Magic: The Gathering™

Dominating Dominia

A Type II Tournament Player's Guide for Magic: The Gathering™

George H. Baxter

Wordware Publishing, Inc.

1506 Capital Avenue

Plano, Texas 75074

Library of Congress Cataloging-in-Publication Data

Baxter, George, 1972-
    Dominating Dominia : a Type II tournament player's guide for
    Magic, the gathering / George H. Baxter.
    p.   cm.
    Includes index.
    ISBN 1-55622-491-5 (pb)
    1. Magic: The Gathering (Game).   I. Title.
    GV1469.62.M34B38   1996
    793.93'2--dc20   96-2014
                                   CIP

ISBN 1-55622-491-5
10 9 8 7 6 5 4 3 2 1
9602

All inquiries for volume purchases of this book should be addressed to Wordware
Publishing, Inc., at 1506 Capital Avenue, Plano, Texas 75074. Telephone inquiries
may be made by calling:

(214) 423-0090

Contents

Thanks to

Sally Spratlen, whose love and support makes my life such a pleasure.

Regan Reece for sifting through my scribble of a manuscript and making it into a book.

My family for their supportive efforts.

The Game Chest and its staff for their help and advice.

Martha McCuller, who saved me many hours by helping with the list in the back.

Adam Maysonet, Chris Pantages, Brian Wiseman, and Henry Stern, whose guidance has been priceless.

This book is dedicated to my grandfather,
George S. Hiland,
after whom I was named.

The illustrations in this book were created by
Christopher Pickrell of Heath, Ohio.

Foreword

by Adam Maysonet

Magic: The Gathering™ is an excellent card game that almost anyone can play. This is because of the simple and straightforward game mechanics. Don't be fooled though. Although it might not be hard to learn how to play, it is very difficult to truly master the nuances of the game.

The game is full of strategy and card combinations that might be old news to you, but other players will be discovering them for the first time. You could end up playing against someone who uses a certain card in a way you've never thought of, or you might possibly stumble upon a combination by accident. A good example of this would be casting Jokulhaups with a Rukh Egg in play on your side, and then seeing the pleasing results after everything is destroyed, while you receive a 4/4 flying Rukh.

Players compete mainly for fun, ante, and tournaments. Some people don't care if they win or lose but instead play for the experience of it. Others, who have a lot of faith in their deck, like to have something at stake, so they put up cards for ante. There is also a large group of players who like to compete in organized tournaments against other people they have never met before. The prize for winning one of these is usually very good, but doing so isn't easy.

Some people, like myself, have learned the finer points by playing other excellent players. To defeat these worthy opponents, you must strive to make a deck that defeats theirs. This induces a process of experimenting that will lead you to a better understanding of the game.

Not everyone has the luxury of being surrounded by competent players, and instead they are stuck in an area where the overall playing level is low. By increasing your own level of play, you will raise the level of skill in your own area as your opponents begin this experimentation process in order to defeat you. This will lead to more challenging and fun duels and raise the level of play even further.

Dominating Dominia will help you succeed in doing all of this. Its main focus is on Type II tournaments, because that is now the dominant tournament type and the fairest to all players. Not everyone has a full set of Moxen, a Black Lotus, Time Walk, etc. to play with. But it's not as difficult to get most of the cards available for use in Type II, because the majority of these cards are still floating around and aren't nearly as expensive.

Inside this book, you will find a plethora of deck listings and instructions on how to play them effectively, strategies for use in Type II settings, and other helpful hints, all of which will prove invaluable to your card playing experience. By using a design from this book, you will not only have a deck that will bring you to victory, but through its use you will discover aspects of the game and deck construction that have previously eluded you. This could lead to you winning more cards, gaining respect as the local guru of Magic, and quite possibly a major tournament victory, like the World Championship.

As a final word to all aspiring players: Good luck, and may your Atogs never be hungry!

Adam Maysonet
Southeast Regional Champion, 1995

Introduction

Dominating Dominia is the first book ever written strictly about Type II Magic. There have been a number of strategy guides written on Magic, but none concentrate on Type II. It was my desire to generate an easy-to-read text that explains all of the nuances of Type II strategy.

From the start, the plan was to produce a text written with clarity and precision for Type II tournament players. *Dominating Dominia* picks up where *Deep Magic* left off: with Type II deck construction. The new material in *Dominating Dominia* on deck construction pertains to the Type II structure. Some technical terms expressed within this volume are from *Deep Magic*. To avoid reader confusion, a recap chapter is included to aid you with any unfamiliar terms that might appear in descriptions of the various decks.

There are over forty decks listed herein with descriptions and advice for playing them, comprising the main body of this book. The decks are the creations of tournament players like Henry Stern (third at World, second at Nationals), Adam Maysonet (Southeastern Regional Champion), Brian Wiseman (creator of "the Deck"), and Mark Justice (American Champion). *Dominating Dominia* will provide you with competitive decks, and then guide you through concepts such as the strategic analysis of attritional deck construction, playing techniques, confronting the Metagame, playing with three or four colors, and fast mana available in Type II.

My desire with this addition to the series, as with all the previous books on Magic, is to increase the deck construction and playing skill of all Magic players. What one person learns from this book transmits to his opponents through the natural course of game playing. My hope is that Magic players as a whole will rise to a new tier in their mastery of the game.

Cry havoc and let slip the dogs of war!

William Shakespeare, *Hamlet*

Chapter 1:

Deep Magic Recap

There are a number of technical terms in this book to describe decks. Most of these terms appear in *Deep Magic: Advanced Strategies for Experienced Players of Magic: The Gathering*. This chapter is a recap of *Deep Magic*. Although I never enter into great detail on technical terms here, they should be clear enough in their own context. If you have already read *Deep Magic*, you may wish to skip this chapter.

Card Economy

The most important concept to master for effective deck construction, as well as effective gameplay, is **card economy**. Card economy is a measurement for determining the effectiveness of decks, combination relationships, and even individual cards. It is essentially a rating of value of a specific card or group of cards, versus the negative aspects of utilizing them. There are three different types of card economy ratings: **card count**, **utility**, and **turn economy**. Each of these terms relates to the others, however there are recognizable differences between them. Sometimes, they are in direct opposition to each other. Designing effective decks often hinges on negotiating tradeoffs between each of these terms of card economy.

Card Count Economy

The first type of card economy is **card count economy**. Card count economy is the measure of how many of your cards you are utilizing compared to how many of your opponent's cards they affect in some way. In this rating, you count the number of cards you employ to remove or disable an opponent's card or put a card in play. The driving concept is to remove two or more of your opponent's cards at the cost of one of your own. Thus, to achieve good card economy, you seek cards which remove as many of your opponent's cards as possible. Some cards like Balance, Wrath of God, and Nevinyrral's Disk carry a high potential for card count economy.

Card count economy is very important to assess in Hand Destruction decks. In these types of decks you seek to force your opponent to lose as many cards from his or her hand as possible at the least expense to yourself. This makes the Mind Twist a powerful card, and thus it is banned under convocation rules. At a cost of one card to yourself you can remove your opponent's entire hand at once. Hymn to Tourach presents a more reasonable trade, but still maintains a 2:1 card ratio since your opponent must discard two cards for each Hymn you play.

Another element of card count economy involves the concept of **draw strength**. If you draw more cards relative to your opponent, then your count ratio is higher. Thus, you can expend more cards against your opponent for an equal effect. Cards like the Jayemdae Tome may be used to increase a deck's draw strength. An increased **draw strength** in a deck allows you to use more cards for the same effect, meaning that you may be able to work with a less efficient card count economy.

Utility

Utility is the second form in measuring card economy. Utility is the measure of a card's effectiveness on the game. Some cards hold a very high utility at certain points in the game, and low utility at other points. For instance, if you cast a Stone Rain late in the game when both players own a relatively high number of effective mana producers, and eliminate one of your opponent's numerous

Mountains, you experience a low level of utility for your employment of that card. However, if you are able to utilize it early in the game on your opponent's only Mountain while he suffers to Vise damage, then you have achieved a much higher card utility.

Most cards exhibit varying levels of utility at different points in the game. For example, a Dark Ritual has a very high level of utility early in the game. However, after the first three turns, the Dark Ritual's power decreases and continues to lessen as the game progresses. Of course, as Marx said, everything solid melts into air, and the Dark Ritual's utility can increase if your opponent is, for example, playing Land Destruction. Conversely, some cards with large casting costs, such as Shivan Dragons, merit greater value later in the game when more mana exists for casting them. However, if you draw these cards early, you waste draws since casting them remains unlikely.

What this all boils down to is that you should try to construct a deck that allows you the possibility of casting cards when you draw them. It is for this reason that cards like Howling Mines provide a great benefit to certain decks. A Small Creature deck experiences more benefit from a Howling Mine than a Burn deck that relies heavily on red X damage spells. The player with the Small Creature deck will typically cast each card drawn, while the player with a red X burn deck will flounder with multiple cards in his hand, not able to use them effectively on the same turn.

The idea of card utility also closely relates with the concept of inter-card relationships. When the cards in your deck connect and fortify each other, you profit more utility from each card in your deck. This means that from drawing the same number of cards, you reap more utility and thus achieve more potency than if the cards were utilized individually. For example, if you use Ashnod's Altar and Living Lands together, by tapping and then sacrificing Forests as creatures you gain three mana for each one. If the Living Lands is in play and you cast the Altar, your Altar has a higher utility than it would on its own, and thus you glean more from your one card than the card's intrinsic value. The act of utilizing better card count economy will not suffice if your opponent can create significantly better card utility from his fewer cards.

Turn Economy

Turn economy is an estimation of how effectively you use each turn. When two equally matched players and decks meet, usually the deciding factor is who goes first. Going first equates to taking an extra Time Walk. I once argued with the Type I National Champion Chip Hogan about the importance of going first. Chip told me that it hardly made any difference if your deck was solid enough. I had to disagree. If you are playing a Vise deck, going first means you enjoy the ability to Vise an opponent on the first turn. If a Counterspell deck faces a Hand Destruction deck, it could be the difference between Power Sinking the Hymn or suffering to it. While players like Chip would be hard pressed to admit it, matches between skilled players often turn on luck and a couple of points of damage. Frequently, those couple of points and that luck result from going first.

Turn economy is important. Turns are another measurement to judge the economy of a deck. If you must consume an entire turn to perform one action and your opponent effectively reacts to the action you took while simultaneously performing another action during his turn, then he enjoys greater turn economy than you. In short, he undoes your turn and maximizes his own.

Consider this scenario. On your first turn you play a Swamp and cast a Dark Ritual and a Hypnotic Specter. Your opponent follows on his turn with a Swamp and also casts a Dark Ritual, a Paralyze on the Hypnotic Specter, and a Knight of Stromgald. In doing this your opponent enjoys both turn and card count economy. Casting the Paralyze and the Knight of Stromgald, he benefits from turn economy. You, on the other hand, cast one card, a Hypnotic Specter. He also experiences card count economy because he effectively eliminated the two cards you cast, a Hypnotic Specter and a Dark Ritual, with one, a Paralyze. In essence, your opponent negates your turn and advances his own deck by emerging a Knight ahead.

There are some cards that can increase your turn economy by denying your opponent the ability to perform actions during his turn. These cards are **environmental cards** like Stasis and Winter Orb. These cards decrease your opponent's ability to act and should not hurt your deck if you recognize the thrust of its own function, the environmental cards themselves. Thus, you can gain turns on your opponent by creating an environment hostile to his development, and simultaneously ambivalent to your own development.

Action Philosophy

The best way to describe **action philosophy** is that an action-based deck is typically cut to eliminate an opponent before he has an opportunity to eliminate you. Action philosophy typically falls under **fast deck theory**, but the two should not be confused. The action philosophy is not centered around speed but around forcing an opponent to react to its actions without trying to compensate for the actions of an opponent. Action philosophy can be looked at as a kind of all out assault on an opponent. Defense is not a high priority under this kind of philosophy.

Reaction Philosophy

Reaction is, as you would probably guess, just the opposite of action philosophy. Reaction decks focus on eliminating threats to establish security, and then initiate action. Reaction decks maintain dominance through control of the environment and by effective removal of obstacles. These decks are usually more versatile than action decks but suffer from a lack of speed. Basically, these decks seek to thwart all of an opponent's assaults and then counterattack once an opponent is disarmed.

Denial Philosophy

Denial philosophy concentrates on denying an opponent the availability of resources. Denial decks usually operate by eliminating an opponent's mana production or forcing an opponent to discard cards from his hand. Denial decks resemble reaction decks because they usually do not mount an assault until an opponent's resources have been depleted to a point where the denial deck maintains control of the environment. There are exceptions to this, but it generally represents the cornerstone of a denial-based deck.

Minor Philosophies

Roads to Victory

When constructing a deck it is wise to understand just how the deck will achieve victory in a duel. The methods for winning a duel are called roads to victory. Roads to victory commonly vary from one deck to another. Action decks may have multiple roads to victory, while reaction decks may operate with only a few. In an action deck, there are usually so many roads to victory that an opponent cannot cut them all off since such a high percentage of the deck is devoted to attack. In reaction and denial decks there are a limited number of roads to victory, but they are well protected by the deck's primary themes. That is, by the time these slower decks begin to attack, the opponent should be in no condition to oppose them. Generally, you should always work to maintain many roads to victory, since many will vanish, and the more that exist, the more likely the deck is to succeed.

Some decks spread out their roads to victory with many different weak sources, and others condense them in a few, very powerful sources. For example, the W&P Tome deck spreads its roads to victory out among several different creatures, instants, and sorcery. The White Vise Age deck gathers its roads to victory into its four Vises and Fireballs. The W&P Tome deck is not greatly affected if some of its roads to victory are cut because it simply lays more roads. Each creature in the deck is one road to victory, and it is difficult for an opponent to deal with each one. The White Vise Age deck relies on its limited sources of victory but has the capability to protect them with a great deal of mana denial. This deck seeks to use one road which is more powerful and better protected; however, if an opponent circumvents this protection then the deck loses a significant amount of its killing power.

One should always consider how many roads to victory his deck possesses and how fragile each of those roads is. Once you estimate your roads to victory, it will assist you in deck play. You will assimilate a better sense of when to start to lay your roads and how to maintain them. The proper management and maintenance of the roads to victory in a deck is absolutely necessary to succeed in a duel.

Surprise Value

Many players load their decks down with four of a card important to the deck in order to pad the statistics of drawing a card or combinations of the cards. Frequently, a player tries this to ensure deck consistency and to attempt to make the deck as predictable as possible. There is a flaw to this strategy. A thoughtful opponent will start to know what to expect from the deck, and as such will play against it better in each successive duel and, moreover, in each successive turn.

If, instead, you add one or two of a certain type of card, your opponent will make decisions based around what they have seen your deck do. This can be very advantageous for you. He may tap out to cast a Fireball, and you can react with an unexpected Power Sink. He may attack with a Blood Lusted, Giant Growthed Llanowar Elves only to find it unexpectedly Unsummoned. Also, if these cards are used early in the game, he may think that you have four of each of them in your deck. For instance, if your opponent casts a Hymn to Tourach on the second turn and you cast your only Power Sink to counter it, he may make future decisions on the assumption that you have more Power Sinks. You can exacerbate this for your opponent by acting discouraged because he will not tap out.

Chapter 2:

New Strategies

This brief chapter explains some of the new strategies that I observed since the writing of *Deep Magic*. The basic concepts behind these theories are the same for both Type I and Type II, though some differences exist because of the differences in the card pools. Both of these theories relate to how you play cards your deck possesses en masse, and the value of using only one or two of a certain card type in your deck.

Attrition Theory

Attrition theory burgeons from the concept of making an opponent use one reactive card to remove each active card you play. Your opponent will almost always have fewer reactive cards than you have active cards in your deck. As an active player in this situation, your goal is to wear down an opponent's defenses by ensuring that they never attain better than one-for-one removal of your cards. By practicing attrition tactics, you force an opponent to deal with each card as it is cast. This strategy also forces an opponent to make decisions about the importance of each card he wishes to remove.

For example, suppose you play against an opponent with a White/Blue deck that uses Wrath of God. You may consider playing one creature at a time against him to force him to deal with each creature individually. If your hand overflows with creatures and you feel compelled to add more to the assault, then proceed if you feel that you received a fair return on your last creature. Observe the following example: you attack your opponent with a White Knight and deal two points of damage. If you decide to cast a second Knight and your opponent responds with a Wrath of God, you can estimate that you dealt two damage for the net of one card. This is because your opponent used a card to eliminate two of yours, but one of your cards contributed to your goal, reducing your opponent's life total to zero.

Perhaps the most formidable type of card to use to minimize your opponent's capacity for removal is artifacts. Only three cards in Type II can remove artifacts en masse. Those three cards are the Jokulhaups, Nevinyrral's Disk, and the Energy Flux. If you play with white, the Disenchant suffices to remove two of these. The average deck contains about three artifact removal cards.

Consider attrition theory as you browse through the decks herein. You may find the theory interesting as you play these decks against different opponents. Many of them seem to fall under attrition theory parameters, while others do not. You should observe how long individual cards stay in play and their quantity in the deck.

Nuisance Theory

A different route to follow in deck construction is to add two or three of a certain card type that an opponent cannot easily deal with. For example, if you play with a creature deficient deck and add two large and threatening creatures, this forces your opponent to either abandon his anti-creature spells, or suffer when he draws them and no creature materializes to play them on. Two large creatures do not necessitate four Swords to Plowshares. His alternative is to remove the anti-creature spells and suffer because he cannot react to the creatures. If, on the other hand, your opponent tries to match the number of creatures you have in the deck with the same number of reactive spells, it will stand as less likely that he will draw them when he needs them.

Chapter 3:

Fast Mana in Type II

Fast Mana Sources in Type II

Land
1. FE Sacrifice Lands
2. FE Storage Lands

Artifacts
1. Ashnod's Altar
2. Fellwar Stone
3. Ice Cauldron
4. Implements of Sacrifice
5. Jeweled Amulet
6. Mana Batteries
7. Mana Vault

White
1. Land Tax

Blue
1. Apprentice Wizard
2. Drain Power
3. Energy Tap
4. High Tide
5. Iceberg

Red
1. Mana Flare
2. Orcish Lumberjack
3. Sisters of the Flame

Black
1. Basal Thrull
2. Burnt Offering
3. Dark Ritual
4. Songs of the Damned
5. Spoils of Evil

Green
1. Birds of Paradise
2. Fyndhorn Elder
3. Fyndhorn Elves
4. Juniper Order Druid
5. Ley Druid
6. Llanowar Elves
7. Nature's Lore
8. Renewal
9. Tinder Wall
10. Untamed Wilds
11. Wild Growth

In Type II, fast mana is not as abundant as it is in Type I (consider the Moxen, Black Lotus, and Sol Ring). This chapter is a summarization of the fast mana sources in Type II Magic and the difficulties involved with using them. This information should assist you when you need to speed your deck up a bit or provide some added punch. An important adjective utilized here is reliability. My definition of reliability refers to table life, or how easily an opponent can remove the card.

Land

Sacrifice Lands

The only lands that provide fast mana for the Type II environment are the sacrifice lands (sack lands) and the storage lands. Sack lands are the Fallen Empires lands that enter play tapped and can be tapped for their regular mana or tapped and sacrificed to produce two of a color. Specifically, the sack lands are the Havenwood Battleground, the Ruins of Trokair, the Dwarven Ruins, the Ebon Stronghold, and the Svyelunite Temple. These lands can assist in casting a creature early, but they are also a nuisance when you draw them as your only land on your first turn and you want to cast a spell. They are also troublesome when you require a land to cast a large spell in a turn, but you draw a sack land instead. This sets you back one turn. This aside, these lands are beneficial if you operate with a two- or three-color deck that has several cards that require two or more of a specific color in their casting cost.

Storage Lands

The storage lands from Fallen Empires are less useful than the sack lands. Storage land decks are, for the most part, useless. This is because they take a long time to accumulate enough counters to make them worthwhile. If drawn in the mid or late game these lands are completely useless. In the early game, players try to leap on their opponents and gain an early advantage. This is not easily accomplished when trying to accumulate storage counters.

Artifacts

Ashnod's Altar

This card represents one of the more underrated cards among tournament players. If you play with any strain of Small Creature/Burn deck, this card can devastate opponents. A measly three creatures in play can convert to six mana in Ashnod's operating room. If that mana combines with the mana provided from your land, it can create a massive Fireball to crush an opponent.

Fellwar Stone

The Fellwar Stone is one of the best forms of fast mana available in Type II. The Stone can be very valuable when you need a constant source of artifact mana. First, it is the best form of alternate artifact mana when playing with Winter Orbs. Second, the Stones work well when playing three- or four-color decks. In many cases it will provide a color you require. Last, the Stone is an efficacious skull crusher when using red or white, because these are the most popular colors in Type II.

Ice Cauldron

Players tend to overrate this card from the Ice Age set. The only logical use I can conceive is in a multi-player game.

Implements of Sacrifice

The Implements of Sacrifice's worth fails to justify its cost, although it could prove rewarding in a Counterspell deck. In such a deck, maybe you could leave one mana untapped and let your opponent believe you are unable to Counterspell for the turn. Maybe not.

Jeweled Amulet

The Jeweled Amulet is a strong card in many multicolored decks that require two of a specific color to cast a number of spells. For example, if you have a Counterspell/Hand Destruction deck, and employ both Hymns to Tourach and Counterspells, you will definitely want to use the Amulet. There are, however, two disadvantages to the Amulet. The greatest disadvantage is that you can only use it every other turn at best. The other disadvantage is that you have to load it, which ties up a mana source.

Mana Batteries

These are too expensive for what they provide. The only way I can conjecture using them is in a Manabarbs deck. In that instance, you can load it turn after turn with alternative sources of mana. Otherwise, it's worthless.

Mana Vault

The Mana Vault is one of the most underrated cards in Magic. Many people play with the Serendib Efreet and the Juzam Djinn in Type I, and they do not worry about the one point of damage per round. The Mana Vault provides a similar circumstance. With a Mana Vault, you can cast a Serra Angel on the second turn or a Mahamoti Djinn on the third. Three turns later you can untap it and others you draw to use them for a massive Fireball in the mid game.

White

Land Tax

While Land Tax contributes no fast mana, it enables you to lay a land each turn. In actuality, this considerably speeds up a deck. Once you "tax out" all of your land, you draw spells for the remainder of the game with enough land to cast them. Land Tax is strong because it works well against Land Destruction and Hand Destruction. If you manage to get both a Zuran Orb and a Land Tax into play you can maintain a full hand and ensure that your opponent's land destruction and hand destruction will never be a threat.

Blue

Apprentice Wizard

The Apprentice Wizard exists for those who want to cast Colossuses of Sardia and Leviathans. Please note the sarcasm in the previous sentence. Apprentice Wizards tap with a cost of one blue mana to provide three colorless mana. These cards are generally a waste of time in a tournament deck. As with all creature mana, opponents easily eliminate them and they are totally unreliable.

Drain Power

Drain Power occasionally merits inclusion in a deck but usually wastes card space. If you add it to a Manabarbs deck, it can severely hurt an opponent. Otherwise, forget it exists. As many tournament players work with Mishra's Factories, they will easily evade a Drain Power by sinking all of their mana into a Factory as a fast effect. (See Chapter 7 for Factories' use as mana dumps.)

Energy Tap

I must declare this for the world to hear: I actually like Energy Tap. While you will not encounter it in many tournament decks, I think it has potential. I used it before in a multi-player game with Balduvian Hydras, casting Energy Tap on one Hydra to cast a larger one. Though this tactic is a waste of time in a tournament deck, it is pure, unadulterated, mindless fun in a multi-player game.

High Tide

This is one of the two blue fast mana cards I would consider using in a tournament deck. In a Blue/Red Burn deck, this card might help to eliminate an opponent more quickly.

Iceberg

The Iceberg is a semi-powerful Type II card. Because it's an enchantment it works well in a Jokulhaups deck. I observed its use in a Type II Obsianus Golem/Jokulhaups/Mana Vault/Iceberg deck. The deck was only Tier Two. Notwithstanding, I believe that the card has potential.

Red

Mana Flare

The Mana Flare's popularity wavers, seemingly with each passing day. The card symbolizes a double-edged sword. In favorable scenarios it will win you the game; in others it betrays you, providing the speed your opponent needs to pulverize you. Mana Flares seldom surface in tournament finals. Think about it.

Orcish Lumberjack

The Orcish Lumberjack is one of the most effective sources of fast creature mana. It permits you to generate four mana for the cost of one Forest. To produce mana in this manner, tap the Forest and sacrifice it to the Lumberjack.

Sisters of the Flame

Two red mana and one other is simply too expensive a price for creature mana. I found it useful in a few sealed deck tournaments; perhaps you will as well.

Black

Basal Thrull

Basal Thrulls are mediocre creatures that cost a reasonable amount of mana. No instances spring to mind, however, where I rushed to include these in a black deck before I included my Hypnotic Specters.

Burnt Offering

This is a serviceable card for a Large Creature/Burn deck. Frequently, these cards can provide the kick to eliminate an opponent. I once witnessed a player crucify an opponent in three turns. On the first turn, he laid a City of Brass and used two Dark Rituals to cast a Vampire. On the second turn, he attacked with the Vampire, played a Dwarven Ruin, and Bolted his opponent with mana from the City of Brass. The opponent was down seven. On the third turn, he laid another land and attacked with his Vampire. The opponent was down eleven. After the attack phase he cast a Dark Ritual and a Burnt Offering on his Vampire. He then sacrificed his Ruin for two mana and tapped the City, pooling a total of ten mana. With the ten mana he cast a nine-point Disintegrate to cremate his opponent. Do not expect a draw as unbelievable as this one, but remember that Burnt Offerings hasten victory.

Dark Ritual

If black is your color, this is the early game fast mana to include. This card's value deteriorates significantly as turns pass. In the mid and late game, drawing this card will annoy you. In many situations it becomes a burden, like excess land. A personal rule I adhere to is to incorporate at least one late game sink for excess mana. Whether it is a Drain Life or a Fireball, it denotes wisdom that a deck contain something for extra Dark Rituals.

Songs of the Damned

This card can support a Black Weenie Creature deck. In the late game, it is likely to produce considerable amounts of black mana. By linking this card with Drain Life, you can sometimes finish an opponent, or at least puncture a bloated life total. Unfortunately, it's weak in the early game.

Spoils of Evil

Though I have not seen it used, I believe this card would function well in a Nevinyrral's Disk/Hand Destruction/Burn deck. If you manage to cast a number of artifacts and creatures into an opponent's graveyard, you can generate a great deal of life and mana with this card. It is weak in the early game.

Green

Birds of Paradise

Green owns multitudes of creature mana. Perhaps the most popular is the Birds of Paradise. The Birds are nice in multi-color decks, but they are unreliable. Many players target the Birds early, operating under the assumption that you need the fast mana.

Fyndhorn Elder

There are many fans and proponents of the Elder, but I am not one of them. The Elder is just too expensive for my taste. Usually when I exploit fast mana, I want it to be fast. The Elder is not only unreliable creature mana, he is also slow. There are many other methods in green to provide fast mana besides the Elder.

Fyndhorn Elves

These cards are decent. I approve of the Elves not only because they provide mana, but because they are damage-dealing creatures. The

Fyndhorn Elves, the Llanowar Elves, and the Orcish Lumberjack are the best of the mana-producing creatures.

Juniper Order Druid

The Juniper Order Druids' cost exceeds their utility for the mana they provide. If they appear with Wild Growth, they can provide a great deal of fast mana. In comparison with other sources of fast mana, I still dole them a low ranking.

Ley Druid

Same as Juniper Order Druid.

Llanowar Elves

Same as the Fyndhorn Elves.

Nature's Lore

This card tops my personal favorites. While it provides you with an extra land on the second turn, it also thins out your deck. I find it problematic to play with a large amount of green and not employ this card. It also works well with a Sylvan Library.

Renewal

Renewal is not a bad card. It works as a double cantrip (spell). You give up a land to cast it but the land is replaced and you draw an extra land. This card is slightly expensive, but it could be of great help in a multi-color deck. Like Nature's Lore, this works well with a Sylvan Library.

Tinder Wall

The Tinder Wall is a unique fast mana source. It is great for casting cards like Ball Lightning and the Ernham Djinn on the second turn. The Wall is a strong card because it acts as both a fast mana source and as a defensive obstacle. One can often use the Wall to smash such pests as Black Knights.

Untamed Wilds

This was one of the first cantrips. I find this a little expensive for what it accomplishes, but in some cases it may prove useful. Like Renewal and Nature's Lore, this works well with Sylvan Library.

Wild Growth

This is a wonderful card if your opponent plays no land destruction. Land destruction causes problems. If an opponent strips out a land and destroys the Wild Growth with it, he nets a two-for-one card count economic advantage. Consider, however, that Wild Growth is slightly more reliable than the Llanowar or Fyndhorn Elves.

Fast Mana Conclusion

Type II possesses little reliable fast mana. Most of the reliable sources are artifacts, which function better than the creature fast mana. The creature fast mana is susceptible to cards like Earthquake and Pyroclasym. Many of the one-shot mana producers provided in black are either feeble in the late game or in the early game. When you are building a deck and you require sources of fast mana, question what you need it for and weigh the importance of its reliability.

Chapter 4:

The Tier Theory of Deck Ranking

The Tier theory of deck ranking is a method for evaluating the competitiveness of different decks and deck types within the Swiss system. Many players use the Tier theory to classify the decks that they encounter. Tier theory is a convenient model to apply to the hordes of decks that players construct daily in the world of Magic. It represents the line between the skull crushers and the crushed skulls.

Tier One Decks

There are four tiers in Tier theory. Tier One decks are those that consistently reach the semifinals. Obviously, most players strive to produce these decks. These decks will beat each of the five basic decks at least sixty percent of the time. A relatively small number of Tier One decks exist among Magic players.

Tier Two Decks

Tier Two decks are decks that are competent, but either lose consistently to one of the five basic decks or fail to achieve the consistency to make it to the semifinals. Frequently, these decks are a version of one of the five basic decks. In some cases, these decks are the clay awaiting transformation by the sculptor's hands into a strong Tier One deck.

Tier Three Decks

Tier Three decks are those that have some coherent strategy behind them but lack the polish to compete. These are decks that new players experiment with as they improve their skill. Common cards you might see in these decks are Dragon Whelps, Dwarven Warriors, Royal Assassins, and Icatian Money Changers.

Tier Four Decks

Tier Four decks are used by new players who have little or no concept of deck construction, or the utterly hopeless. Children and those new to the game play these decks. Typically, their decks contain such favorites as Creature Bonds, Gray Ogres, and Pearled Unicorns. After you finish splattering these decks' intestines hither and yon, please do a favor to the Magic community and inform these people what is wrong with their decks.

A Note

After witnessing, participating in, and analyzing over forty Type II tournaments, I conclude that it is a rarity for a highly reactive deck type (e.g., Millstone deck) to reach the first tier. The only tournament I ever participated in where a reactive deck was victorious was Mage Wars in Tyler, Texas. There, the victor of the tournament won with the Engine deck in Chapter Nine.

I believe that reactive decks do not perform as well in Type II as in Type I because there are fewer cards that kill active decks in Type II than in Type I. Type I holds the Abyss and the Moat. The only card in Type II that compares with these is the Island Sanctuary; not nearly as powerful as a Moat or the Abyss. Reactive decks are starting to undergo an upswing though due to the restriction of the Black Vise.

Chapter 5:

Confronting the Metagame

What in the heck is the Metagame? Well, the Metagame consists of the parameters under which you play. These parameters can be vague, like the Type II Duelists' Convocation rules, or as exact as knowing the composition of your opponent's deck.

Perhaps the best example I can provide you with to familiarize you with the Metagame is Mark Justice's victory at the National Championship in 1995. Mark Justice, from Salt Lake City, Utah, managed to win because he took a risk. Mark constructed his deck on information about the decks his opponents played. He understood the composition of the Metagame. He reconnoitered his competition in previous rounds, seeing that his opponents would rely heavily on artifacts, and accordingly used several anti-artifact cards. He knew that several of his opponents played black Hand Destruction decks, so he prepared for them with Whirling Dervishes and Lifeforces. This is why it is often wise to bring two different decks, especially if you are confident you will qualify and move to the finals.

Note: At the time of the 1995 National Championship, Zuran Orb and Black Vise were not restricted and Channel was not banned.

Mark Justice's National Championship 1995 Deck

Block 1	Block 2	Block 3
Pocket 1	Pocket 1	Pocket 1
Whirling Dervish	Strip Mine	Karplusan Forest
Whirling Dervish	Strip Mine	Karplusan Forest
Whirling Dervish	Strip Mine	Karplusan Forest
Whirling Dervish	Strip Mine	Karplusan Forest
Pocket 2	Pocket 2	Pocket 2
Lifeforce	Johtull Wurm	Mountain
Lifeforce	Zuran Orb	Mountain
Shivan Dragon	Zuran Orb	Mountain
Orgg	Channel	Mountain
Pocket 3	Pocket 3	Pocket 3
Incinerate	Tranquility	Forest
Incinerate	Pyroclasym	Forest
Incinerate	Pyroclasym	Forest
Incinerate	Timberline Ridge	Forest
Pocket 4	Pocket 4	Pocket 4
Lighting Bolt	Crumble	Mountain
Lighting Bolt	Crumble	Mountain
Lighting Bolt	Crumble	Mountain
Lighting Bolt	Crumble	Mountain
Pocket 5	Pocket 5	Pocket 5
Black Vise	Fireball	Forest
Black Vise	Fireball	Forest
Ivory Tower	Fireball	Forest
Rack	Fireball	Forest

Sideboard

1. Pyroclasym
2. Pyroclasym
3. Earthquake
4. Earthquake
5. Rack
6. Hurricane
7. Lifeforce
8. Lifeforce
9. Tranquility
10. Tranquility
11. Jayemdae Tome
12. Disrupting Scepter
13. Disrupting Scepter
14. Shatter
15. Shatter

After the tournament, Justice said that he took the risk and played against his opponents instead of sticking to his best deck. The lesson learned is that one should try to avoid playing a singular deck and construct another so an opponent cannot prepare beforehand. Justice displayed his mastery of the Metagame.

The Metagame of the Swiss Style and Single Elimination

The Swiss Style

The Swiss style is a form of tournament play in which players compete with one another to accumulate points. After a number of matches, the judges tally the points and determine a winner or choose a finalist for the semifinal and final matches.

Swiss tournaments are usually timed. Typically, each player receives fifteen minutes per game. This puts many slow decks at a great disadvantage. Most of the successful decks in the Swiss style are active decks.

In Swiss style tournaments, you play a set number of games for each match, usually three. You earn points for the games, not for the match. In comparison, the winner of a Duelists' Convocation match wins two out of three games. This means that the first

Points in the Duelists' Convocation—Swiss	
Win	3 Points
Loss	0 Points
Draw	1 Point each
Unfinished	0 Points

game is even more important in the Swiss than it is in Single Elimination. Each lost game steals points from your total.

When challenging the Metagame, this has certain implications. If the first game has a greater amount of value, and each game is independent from the others, the sideboard suffers in this format. If you consistently lose your first game, yet are able to overcome any opponent in the second and third game due to an imposing sideboard, you still may not qualify.

The Swiss Gambit

The Swiss Gambit is a method that you can employ to qualify for the finals of a tournament without having to face many challenging players. In order to play the gambit, you need to tie or lose one game in your first round. From that point on you will match up with players with imperfect records. The obvious problem with the gambit is that you lose your previous margin for error.

Single Elimination

In Single Elimination tournaments your sideboard is a much stronger weapon, and these tournaments are not timed. This means that you have a lot of room to exercise a more reactive deck. This style is not as accurate as the Swiss because your bracket does not change with your success. Also, a player's fate depends largely on luck. One bad draw may doom a player to a teeth-grinding, first-round exit.

Taking Advantage of the Metagame

In order to maximize your success in the Metagame, it often helps to have some information about what decks people play. If you attend a local tournament outside of your home town, establish who is the best and what they play. In most cases, all of the other players will use the same type of deck or one that can combat it. The Metagame can destroy your competition, allowing you to recognize the cliff which the other sheep will walk obediently and devotedly off of.

Chapter 6:

The Transition of Type II

There have been a number of changes in the perspective of most of the top players. In the early days of Type II (post-4th Edition), certain cards were considered too powerful for inclusion in the Type II format.

Restrict the Vise?

When I went to Origins for the National Championships in the summer of 1995, everyone feared the Black Vise. When I interviewed Mark Justice and Mike Long they both told me that they believed the Black Vise should be restricted. In the summer of 1995 most tournament players had not yet found a way to overcome the Vise in a reactive deck. Most tournament players believed that certain decks were no longer possible because of the Vise's existence. Mark Justice made the point that no Blue/White Counterspell deck stood a chance with the Vise as unrestricted. At that time, no one had invented a blue/white deck to dispute his point. Eventually, some players took advantage of the large number of zero and one casting cost artifacts available to them. Cards like the Zuran Orb, Fountain of Youth, Urza's Bauble, and Barbed Sextant enhanced decks, allowing them to cast cards and get under the Vise.

People began to realize that the Vise was not a great threat unless an opponent constructed a deck to support it. Many players argued that if the Black Vise appeared on the first turn, it is likely that a player suffered at least six points of damage before he could get under it. This was true, but that damage was only a threat during the early game. If your opponent could not eliminate you in the early game, in the mid and late game any Vises drawn would be useless cards for him. If an opponent had four Vises in his deck, drew a Vise in his first eight cards, played it, and managed to deal six points of damage before you could dispose of enough cards, the damage dealt to you calculated as only one-and-a-half points per Vise.

The Duelists' Convocation declared the Black Vise restricted to one per deck as of February 1, 1996. And from that point the Metagame changed, old doors were sealed shut and new ones opened.

"Braaaaaaack Channel Fireball"
—Pat the Parrot

People want someone to blame for the restriction of the Channel. We could blame the Lumberjack, the Tinder Wall, or even the Zuran Orb, but regardless of where the blame should be laid, Channel grew too obnoxious to tolerate. It became much too easy for a player to engulf his opponent with a massive Fireball on the second turn and chalk up a game to luck. Even in the late game after a player's life total was less, the Channel was still dangerous because of the Zuran Orb. With the Orb out, you could sacrifice all of your land for life to add to the pool for the Channel. The officials at Wizards of the Coast witnessed too many major tournaments won via the Channel Fireball combination, and they wisely restricted Channel.

Zuran Orb: a Silent Death in the Swiss

The Zuran Orb is a constant problem for the Swiss style tournament. Once an opponent's Zuran Orb is in play, not only must you reduce his life to zero, but you must cause two points of damage for each land he plays. This causes problems in the Swiss tournaments, where time limits loom over matches. If two players with defensive decks meet, their match usually ends in a draw which damages both players' overall average. This places the Orb in the same category as the Ivory Tower. Many of the defenders of the Orb argue that it is not the same as the Tower, because the Tower is cumulative and the Orb is redundant, depending on land to feed it. However, the proponents of a non-restricted Zuran Orb fail to recognize that the Orb frequently came four to a deck, and the chances of drawing it are much greater than one Ivory Tower. The Zuran Orb was eventually restricted because of its threat to the integrity of the Swiss system.

A Multiplicity of Legends

If you take a look at the number of Legends in most Tier One tournament decks, you will notice that they do not use Legends. There is no practical reason why the Duelists' Convocation should restrict a deck to one Legend. Recently, some strong Legends joined the card pool. Ice Age added Marton Stromgald; Homelands added the Ihsan's Shade, Autumn Willow, and Eron the Relentless; and Chronicles brought back Sol'kanar and Nebuchadnezzar. Some of these Legends pop up in the most competitive of decks because of the Convocation's lifting of the restriction.

"Oh Look—I Drew My Mind Twist. I Win."

The Mind Twist was the most powerful card in Type II. There was no stronger card. In the tremendous majority of the games that a player successfully cast a Mind Twist, they won. Period. As in, the game is over, you lose. Go home, place your head squarely in a vise, and turn lever to apply pressure. Continue process until drooling and basket weaving become higher priorities for you than playing Magic: The Gathering. This card was well on its way to being banned. Some suggested that if the Psychic Purge returned that the Mind Twist would not be such a threat. This assumption was incorrect. The Mind Twist was a card that could fit into most Type II decks without any other Hand Destruction. The idea of a player loading his deck up with Purges, hoping his opponent would Twist them out, was ludicrous. The likely result for a player would have been four near useless cards in his hand while his opponent bludgeoned his skull. The Mind Twist belonged in a similar category as the Channel.

On January 1, 1996, the Duelists' Convocation placed the Mind Twist in the same category as the Channel. The Mind Twist, as of February 1, 1996, was banned, and good riddance.

Chapter 7:

Disk Decks

The Nevinyrral's Disk is one of the two most powerful artifacts in Type II Magic. The Disk's ability to eliminate all creatures, enchantments, and artifacts in play enables the Disk's controller to reset an opponent's position. When a player constructs a deck

Cards That Function Well in Disk Decks

Land	Artifacts	Blue
1. Ice Floe	1. Barbed Sextant	1. Boomerang
2. Mishra's Factory	2. Nevinyrral's Disk	2. Counterspell
3. Safe Haven	3. Pit Trap	3. Deflection
4. Strip Mine		4. Ghost Ship
		5. Hurkl's Recall
		6. Power Sink

Red	Black	White
1. Disintegrate	1. Ashen Ghoul	1. Blinking Spirit
2. Eron the Relentless	2. Drudge Skeletons	2. Swords to
3. Fireball	3. Foul Familiar	Plowshares
4. Incinerate	4. Hymn to Tourach	
5. Lava Burst	5. Nether Shadow	Green
6. Lightning Bolt		1. Nature's Lore
7. Meteor Shower		2. Storm Seeker
8. Pyrotechnics		
9. Uthden Troll		

around the Nevinyrral's Disk, he will often employ particular cards to overcome the negative aspects associated with the Disk. The negative aspects will be those deriving from the word "all," as in "all creatures, enchantments and artifacts," including your own. Overcoming the negative aspects allows the player of the Disk deck an opportunity to gain a card count economic advantage. Many times, the Disk will eliminate three or four of an opponent's cards in one hellish detonation.

Disks and Regenerators

Some challenges exist to deploying the Disk. A player cannot simply throw four Disks into a deck and expect to enjoy all of the benefits of their presence. There are a number of routes that a player can take to insure that the Disk will produce results. One method to utilize when constructing a Disk deck is to rely on permanents that will not be eliminated by the Disk. These permanents include most regenerating creatures, like the Uthden Troll, Ghost Ship, Eron the Relentless, Will-O-The-Wisp, and Drudge Skeleton.

In order to maximize their effectiveness, a player can blow the Disk during his opponent's end phase to destroy all opposing creatures and regenerate his own. This will give the controller of the Disk deck an opportunity to have his creatures attack without any blockers to stop them. Consider, however, that there are several ways to maintain dominance with permanents other than using regenerators.

Blinkers, Familiars, Unsummons, Ghouls, and Shadows

Another way to protect your creatures from the Disk is to make certain that they are not present when the Disk detonates. This may sound ridiculously obvious, but it is an eminently useful strategy. One method a player may utilize in accomplishing this makes use of those fast effect abilities or spells that return a creature to the player's hand. Blinking Spirits and Foul Familiar's special ability to return to a player's hand as a fast effect allow them protection from the Disk without the expense of casting spells. You can also achieve this for other creatures with the use of Unsummons, Word of Undoing, or Boomerangs. Though this particular strategy can work effectively, it is perhaps best exploited with the Spirits or Familiars. This means a player need not sacrifice a card or spell to save his creatures.

Some Disk decks can function well even if their creatures are sent to the graveyard. This represents the second strategy for protection from Disks. Intelligent players sometimes design decks with Ashen Ghouls and Nether Shadows in coordination with the Disks. Once any combination of four Ghouls and Shadows reach the graveyard, their controller can always maintain a creature in play. Remember, during the upkeep phase, the Shadows and Ghouls have the ability to reenter the game with the presence of three creatures above them and the appropriate mana payment.

These decks also fare well against decks that use a large amount of anti-creature spells, Hand Destruction, or Counterspells. The only cards that truly hurt this type of deck are Swords to Plowshares and Disintegrates. These cards will remove the Ghouls and Shadows from the game instead of placing them in the graveyard, thus effectively countering the basic strategy of the deck.

Disks and Land

The third most common way to avoid the Disk's effect is to use the one permanent that the Disk fails to destroy: land. The plethora of lands in Magic that possess special abilities contribute well to a Disk deck. The most obvious choice of these lands is the Mishra's Factory. After the Disk detonates, the Factories are often the only creatures left on the table. Safe Havens are another alternative. Frequently, you can use a creature in play until an opponent recognizes its nuisance, and decides to terminate it. Now, the Safe Haven's practicality becomes apparent. Once a creature enters Safe Haven, the Disk will not harm it. After the Disk detonates, you simply release the creatures in the Haven back into play. The table now favors you, and you may overwhelm your opponent. Strip Mines can also help because they can eliminate an opponent's more troublesome lands. The last of these functional, special ability lands to add to a Disk deck is the Ice Floe. Often when using a Disk deck, the Disks have a diminishing, marginal utility. The first Disk often destroys several permanents, while the second Disk is more likely to only destroy a few permanents, and the third Disk rarely destroys more than one permanent, if it shows up at all. This diminishing return makes the Ice Floe useful in a Disk deck. Ice Floes lock down an opponent's creatures, confirming that you will receive a one card advantage when the Disk detonates. These special lands often comprise an important element in Disk decks.

Disks and Non-permanents

Many tournament players dismiss constructing Disk decks that rely on permanents. There are several advantages to avoiding the use of permanents. The first advantage is that your opponent will commonly face the predicament of an excess of cards in his hand. This is because an opponent will have reactive cards in his deck, and the absence of permanents prevents him from casting them. This causes him to discard otherwise useful cards, leaving him with an immediate card count disadvantage. This strategy renders cards like Swords to Plowshares, Terror, Tranquility, and Control Magic useless.

The Burn Route

There are a number of routes to shore up a Disk deck. One method, the Burn route, employs the use of non-permanents to inflict damage. The Burn route remains a very popular non-permanent strategy. A Disk deck that relies on the Burn route enjoys many of the tactical advantages of the standard Burn type deck, along with the awesome board clearing potential of the Disk. A common and frequently successful strategy for a controller of a Burn/Disk deck is to hold off his opponent's creatures until the Burn/Disk controller can cast a Disk. After a Disk detonates, the Burn/Disk player will enjoy a card count economic advantage. He will probably have more than enough direct damage to burn any creatures the opponent casts. The player can now control the match for its duration. The probability that land will accumulate as turns progress guarantees the deadliness of red X direct damage spells (Fireball, Disintegrate, and Lava Burst). A player should ponder heavily the X in any red X spell when twelve lands rest quietly in play on his opponent's side.

However, players will observe problems when taking the Burn route. The principal problem is that Burn deck players commonly depend on the cards they have in hand. Players need each card to match an opponent's card in order to overcome them. This makes Hand Destruction decks particularly menacing. If a Hand Destruction deck manages to draw its Hymns and Mind Warps, it can severely cut the chances of success for a Burn/Disk player. Another problem for these decks arises in a well tuned Creature deck. If an opposing player leaves one creature in play at a time, while keeping a reserve of creatures in his hand to replace each creature as it is destroyed by burn spells, that Creature deck's stamina and persistence can outlast a Burn deck. This is because Burn decks must react to Creature decks or confront the steady pain of continuous damage inflicted from a constant source. Most likely, creatures will have the opportunity to attack and deal damage before the opponent removes them. Creatures that deal damage and require the opponent to spend a spell to destroy them shift card economy in the Creature deck controller's favor.

Hand Destruction and Disks

There is a responsive strategy to opponents who hold cards back to avoid losing them to a Disk. Hand Destruction Disk decks effectively dismember hands composed of withheld cards while still threatening permanents with the destructive power of the Disk. If an opponent holds permanents back, you can use Hand Destruction to remove them; if your opponent plays his permanents, then the Disk will eliminate them. The Hand Destruction and Disk combination breaks opponents, frequently leaving them without any options.

However, there are two major weaknesses that this deck type suffers from. First, it is particularly vulnerable to fast creatures, whose quick damage potential demands a player eliminate them. These fast creatures include Hypnotic Specters, Mindstab Thrulls, Savanna Lions, Mishra's Factories, etc. Second, they lack possibilities to defeat an opponent. Not possessing the possibility for victory should leap to your attention as a glaring problem. Obviously, destroying cards will not suffice to provide a road to victory. These decks depend on a secondary theme to provide that road.

Deck Name: The Deal With It Deck

Block One	Block Two	Block Three
Pocket 1	Pocket 1	Pocket 1
Hypnotic Specter	Hymn to Tourach	Sulfurous Springs
Hypnotic Specter	Hymn to Tourach	Sulfurous Springs
Hypnotic Specter	Hymn to Tourach	Sulfurous Springs
Hypnotic Specter	Hymn to Tourach	Sulfurous Springs
Pocket 2	Pocket 2	Pocket 2
Mindstab Thrull	Nevinyrral's Disk	City of Brass
Mindstab Thrull	Nevinyrral's Disk	Swamp
Mindstab Thrull	Nevinyrral's Disk	Swamp
Mindstab Thrull	Nevinyrral's Disk	Swamp
Pocket 3	Pocket 3	Pocket 3
Ashen Ghoul	Disrupting Scepter	Mishra's Factory
Ashen Ghoul	Fireball	Mishra's Factory
Ashen Ghoul	Fireball	Mishra's Factory
Ashen Ghoul	Fireball	Mishra's Factory
Pocket 4	Pocket 4	Pocket 4
Nether Shadow	Dark Ritual	Swamp
Nether Shadow	Dark Ritual	Swamp
Nether Shadow	Dark Ritual	Swamp
Nether Shadow	Dark Ritual	Swamp
Pocket 5	Pocket 5	Pocket 5

Knights of Stromgald	Barbed Sextant	Swamp
Knights of Stromgald	Barbed Sextant	Swamp
Knights of Stromgald	Barbed Sextant	Swamp
Knights of Stromgald	Barbed Sextant	Swamp

Sideboard:

1. Order of the Ebon Hand
2. Order of the Ebon Hand
3. Order of the Ebon Hand
4. Order of the Ebon Hand
5. Tranquility
6. Tranquility
7. Lightning Bolt
8. Lightning Bolt
9. Lightning Bolt
10. Lightning Bolt
11. Shatter
12. Shatter
13. Pyroblast
14. Pyroblast
15. Pyroblast

Use Order of the Ebon Hands for White decks, Tranquilities for C.O.P. Black and Karma, Lightning Bolts for other Hand Destruction decks, Shatters for Artifact intensive decks, and Pyroblasts for Control Magics.

This Hand Destruction Disk deck takes advantage of the Ashen Ghoul and Nether Shadow's ability to return to play from the graveyard. With twenty-four creatures and thirteen hand destruction spells, this deck makes any mage powerful. To begin, the controller of this deck should launch an attack with as many creatures as he can muster in the shortest period of time. After an opponent dumps creatures into play to provide defense against your army, the number of cards in his hand will significantly lessen. The cards that remain will either cost too much to cast, or be reactive cards like Disenchants, Crumbles, or Shatters. Now, use your Hymns to take the remainder of his hand and pitch it into the graveyard. His hand is now empty, providing an opportune time to cast the Disk.

One of the more twisted advantages of detonating the Disk is that you may choose the order in which your cards go to the graveyard. This implies that you could send your Ghouls to the graveyard first, followed by the Nether Shadows, and then the remainder of the creatures. Next upkeep, your opponent faces a stampede of the undead.

Deck Name: The Deal With It Deck II

Block One	Block Two	Block Three
Pocket 1	Pocket 1	Pocket 1
Savanna Lion	Hymn to Tourach	City of Brass
Savanna Lion	Hymn to Tourach	City of Brass
Savanna Lion	Hymn to Tourach	City of Brass
Savanna Lion	Hymn to Tourach	City of Brass
Pocket 2	Pocket 2	Pocket 2
Hypnotic Specter	Swords to Plowshares	Plains
Hypnotic Specter	Swords to Plowshares	Plains
Hypnotic Specter	Swords to Plowshares	Plains
Hypnotic Specter	Swords to Plowshares	Plains
Pocket 3	Pocket 3	Pocket 3
Serra Angel	Barbed Sextant	Swamp
Serra Angel	Barbed Sextant	Swamp
Derelore	Barbed Sextant	Swamp
Derelore	Barbed Sextant	Swamp
Pocket 4	Pocket 4	Pocket 4
Mishra's Factory	Dark Ritual	Swamp
Mishra's Factory	Dark Ritual	Swamp
Mishra's Factory	Dark Ritual	Swamp
Mishra's Factory	Dark Ritual	Swamp
Pocket 5	Pocket 5	Pocket 5
Blinking Spirit	Nevinyrral's Disk	Swamp
Blinking Spirit	Nevinyrral's Disk	Swamp
Blinking Spirit	Nevinyrral's Disk	Swamp
Disrupting Scepter	Nevinyrral's Disk	Swamp

Sideboard:
1. Disenchant
2. Disenchant
3. Disenchant
4. Disenchant
5. Knight of Stromgald
6. Knight of Stromgald
7. Knight of Stromgald
8. Knight of Stromgald
9. Order of the Ebon Hand
10. Deflection
11. Deflection
12. Pyroblast
13. Pyroblast
14. Pyroblast
15. Pyroblast

One of the difficulties with the Red/Black Deal With It deck is its lack of ability to deal with an opponent's permanents without the use of the Disk. This deck can remove an opponent's bothersome permanents without requiring the detonation of the Disk. This deck also contains a greater diversity among its sources of damage. Although the first deck has two separate colors that deal damage, the red X spells exist for creature removal rather than damage. In the Black/White Hand Destruction deck, the Blinking Spirits and Serra Angels provide a more permanent and consistent threat than the Fireballs and the other red/black. Though this deck is less likely to overrun an opponent, it has a greater chance in the mid and late game.

Counterspell Disk Deck

Counterspell Disk decks are similar to Direct Damage Disk decks in many ways. Both deck types allow an opponent to deploy a number of permanents when they cast a Disk. Once the Disk detonates, an opponent plays with a card count disadvantage for the duration of the match.

Additionally, the Counterspell Disk deck shares several of the same problems that appear with the Hand Destruction Disk decks. Like the Hand Destruction Disk decks, the Counterspell Disk deck contains few or no methods for dealing with an opponent's early creatures. Also, Counterspell Disk decks share the Hand Destruction Disk deck's weakness of the need for a secondary theme to provide a road to victory. The Counterspell Disk deck also suffers a speed disadvantage, slowly plodding to initiate control of the match, merged with a controller's tendency to hold cards.

A Counterspell Disk deck rarely plays without either white or red removal as a secondary theme. Although, it is conceivable that a player could construct a Counterspell Hand Destruction Disk deck. Such a deck would suffer from all the problems associated with Counterspell and Hand Destruction deck types.

Deck Name: The Ghost and Toast Deck

Block One	Block Two	Block Three
Pocket 1	Pocket 1	Pocket 1
Nevinyrral's Disk	Counterspell	Island
Nevinyrral's Disk	Counterspell	Island
Nevinyrral's Disk	Counterspell	Island
Nevinyrral's Disk	Counterspell	Island
Pocket 2	Pocket 2	Pocket 2
Lightning Bolt	Power Sink	Island
Lightning Bolt	Power Sink	Island
Lightning Bolt	Power Sink	Island
Lightning Bolt	Recall	Island
Pocket 3	Pocket 3	Pocket 3
Incinerate	Control Magic	Mountain
Incinerate	Control Magic	Island
Ice Floe	Control Magic	Island
Balance	Fireball	Island
Pocket 4	Pocket 4	Pocket 4
Ghost Ship	Barbed Sextant	Mountain
Ghost Ship	Barbed Sextant	Mountain
Ghost Ship	Barbed Sextant	Mountain
Ghost Ship	Barbed Sextant	Mountain
Pocket 5	Pocket 5	Pocket 5
Mishra's Factory	Fireball	Adarkar Wastes
Mishra's Factory	City of Brass	Mountain
Mishra's Factory	City of Brass	Mountain
Mishra's Factory	City of Brass	Mountain

Sideboard:

1. Shatter	6. Hydroblast	11. Pyroclasym
2. Shatter	7. Hydroblast	12. Pyroclasym
3. Shatter	8. Deflection	13. Control Magic
4. Shatter	9. Pyroclasym	14. Pyroblast
5. Hydroblast	10. Pyroclasym	15. Pyroblast

Use the Shatters for heavy Artifact decks and Vise decks, Hydroblasts for Burn decks and Red decks, Deflection for Burn decks or non-permanent decks, Pyroclasyms for small creatures, Control Magic for Large Creature or Hand Destruction decks, and Pyroblasts for Counterspell or Control Magic decks.

This deck resembles the Disk deck I used at the National Championship last year. It did reasonably well in the qualifying rounds, but it was too slow to survive. Though the deck displayed strength in general, it did not function adequately against Vises or against White Weenie decks in the first game. The format of the Nationals Tournament was Swiss, and there were only two games per match. Because individual games counted, and not the matches as a whole, the advantage of a sideboard strategy declined significantly. While this deck will perform well in a single elimination tournament, it falls short in the Swiss style.

The Ghost Ships endow this deck with a lethal nature. Ghost Ships prove quite difficult to eliminate once they come into play. When the Incinerate appeared in the Ice Age edition, regenerating creatures suffered mightily. Ghost Ships, in contrast to other regenerating creatures, did not suffer in usage due to the Incinerate's appearance, providing a great strategic windfall to their user. Their four toughness pushes them out of the range of Incinerates. If an opponent wishes to eliminate a Ghost Ship with an Incinerate, he requires a second direct damage spell to do it, perhaps another Incinerate. This immunity to singular Incinerates compels players to include the Ghost Ship in decks.

Many times late in the game, the Disks became much harder for my opponents to handle. I could usually protect the Disk with counter magic. If I managed to survive the first six turns, and could lay a land each turn, I would consistently take the match. This is because this deck's controller can often cast a Disk and protect it with a Counterspell. This deck depends heavily upon the Disk, but not all Disk decks possess this impairment.

Disk Deck Playing Tactics

There are a number of playing tactics that any Disk deck player should understand. The simplest of these tactics is to hold permanents back instead of playing them immediately while the Disk is in play. This strategy will give the Disk's controller an opportunity to launch an assault after the Disk detonates.

The most challenging aspect of Disk use is knowing when to set it off. In some cases it is best to wait until your opponent declares an attack phase. There are several reasons why you might wait until this point. Frequently, your opponent will foolishly cast permanents before his attack phase. This will provide you the opportunity to eliminate more cards with the Disk and improve your card count advantage. Another reason to wait until your opponent's attack phase is to eliminate more opportunities for your opponent to inflict damage on you. If your opponent has Mishra's Factories or a Ball Lightning, prevent him from using those weapons by blowing the Disk during his attack phase.

In some cases, it is best to detonate the Disk on your turn. Usually, it is more beneficial to blow the Disk when your opponent plays Howling Mines or several artifacts and creatures that he will use continuously if you allow him to untap them on his turn. Frequently, by blowing the Disk on your turn, you can deny your opponent the opportunity to draw an extra card, gain an extra point of life, or inflict an extra point of damage.

Situations might also arise where the best time to use a Disk is at the end of your opponent's turn. Typically, you do this if your opponent is not able to deal any real damage with his creatures. This allows the Disk's controller to maximize the effect of the Disk by forcing his opponent to either cast a card from his hand and lose it to the Disk, or to hold cards back and not glean the benefits of their usage.

Disking Again and Again and Again

In some situations, you may desire to reproduce the Disk's effect with greater frequency than you normally obtain with only four Disks in a deck. A common technique to reproduce a Disk's effect is to use either Boomerangs or Hurkyl's Recalls. When you blow the Disk, you can use these cards to return the Disk to your hand. The Disk still blows, and you have it available to cast again, much to the chagrin of your adversary. When deciding which of these cards to use, remember that Boomerangs have obvious advantages over Hurkyl's Recall. You can use Boomerangs to return any permanent to a player's hand, while Hurkyl's Recall only affects artifacts. This ability to affect all permanents makes them a versatile selection for your deck. However, Hurkyl's Recalls, used selectively, are more effective in specific decks. These specific decks include decks exercising multiple artifacts in play at one time. A player in this situation would want to retrieve all his precious artifacts when the Disk detonates.

Common Problems with Disk Decks

A great truth in Magic is that all decks will contain flaws. It is no surprise then that there are a few problems with Disk decks as a whole. First, sluggishness cripples these decks and makes them a risk in Swiss-style or other timed tournaments. Another problem with the Disk decks is that they are often very light on artifacts, making them very susceptible to anti-artifact spells. The Disks comprise the majority of the artifacts in the Disk deck, and so the deck provides few alternative targets for an opposing deck with anti-artifact spells. If you only have four artifacts in your deck and your opponent has four Disenchants, it is unlikely that the four artifacts in your deck will be effective. The probability of the opponent drawing his anti-artifact Disenchant is equal to you drawing your artifact.

A Blending of the Strategies

More often than not, Disk deck construction strategies blend. Rarely will players construct pure Counterspell Disk decks, Burn Disk decks, or Hand Destruction Disk decks. In most cases, a synthesis of two of these elements emerges. The following decks are all examples of combinations of these deck types.

Adam Maysonet's "DDDD" (Direct Damage Disk Deck)

Block One	Block Two	Block Three
Pocket 1	Pocket 1	Pocket 1
Lightning Bolt	Disenchant	City of Brass
Lightning Bolt	Disenchant	City of Brass
Lightning Bolt	Disenchant	City of Brass
Lightning Bolt	Strip Mine	City of Brass
Pocket 2	Pocket 2	Pocket 2
Incinerate	Nevinyrral's Disk	Dwarven Ruins
Incinerate	Nevinyrral's Disk	Dwarven Ruins
Incinerate	Nevinyrral's Disk	Mountain
Incinerate	Nevinyrral's Disk	Mountain
Pocket 3	Pocket 3	Pocket 3
Disintegrate	Jayemdae Tome	Mountain
Disintegrate	Jayemdae Tome	Mountain
Disintegrate	Strip Mine	Mountain
Disintegrate	Strip Mine	Mountain
Pocket 4	Pocket 4	Pocket 4
Fireball	Mishra's Factory	Mountain
Fireball	Mishra's Factory	Mountain
Fireball	Mishra's Factory	Plains
Fireball	Mishra's Factory	Plains
Pocket 5	Pocket 5	Pocket 5
Swords to Plowshares	Savanna Lions	Plains
Swords to Plowshares	Savanna Lions	Plains
Swords to Plowshares	Savanna Lions	Plains
Balance	Savanna Lions	Plains

Sideboard:

1. Pyroblast	6. Land Tax	11. C.O.P. Red
2. Pyroblast	7. Land Tax	12. C.O.P. Red
3. Pyroblast	8. Pyroclasym	13. C.O.P. Red
4. Swords to Plowshares	9. Pyroclasym	14. Jester's Cap
5. Disenchant	10. Pyroclasym	15. Jester's Cap

Use the Pyroblasts to combat Blue Control decks, Swords to Plowshares against Large Fast Creature decks, Disenchant for artifact heavy decks, Land Taxes for Hand Destruction and Land Destruction, Pyroclasyms for Small Creature decks, C.O.P. Reds for other direct damage decks, and Jester's Caps for Blinking Spirits and sideboard nuisances.

Adam Maysonet has been a fan of the Disk deck ever since the restriction of Balance. When Adam sent me this deck he added a note, "Enjoy, and become mighty and powerful. It's very simple, yet effective." The deck competes well with most decks. With a few exceptions, creature-based decks suffer greatly to the DDDD. The DDDD's sixteen direct damage spells, four Nevinyrral's Disks and four Swords to Plowshares create difficulties for a creature-based deck. Opponents will notice problems keeping a creature in play against the DDDD, as burned and electrocuted corpses pile up in the graveyard. Since Type II remains so creature-oriented, it is not difficult for a deck like the DDDD to dominate. As with most Burn decks, as turns pass and a greater amount of land appears in play, the DDDD's Fireballs and Disintegrates become increasingly powerful. In the early game, the DDDD deck is very reactive, but in the middle to late game it becomes more aggressive and starts to take on an offensive character.

After testing the DDDD, I found it contains a few weaknesses. This particular deck fared pretty poorly against some of the Blue/White Tome decks or Winter Orb decks. The Blue/White Tome decks achieved victory about fifty percent of the time in the first games of matches with the DDDD. If the DDDD's Disks were ever successfully cast, they were often disenchanted immediately after. After both decks sideboarded, a blue/white addition of a C.O.P. Red effectively took the teeth out of the DDDD deck. The C.O.P. Red can often be cast, and frequently appears, in multiples. A player then protects it with counter magic. Blinking Spirits are also a problem for the DDDD because there is no way for it to eliminate them. The Spirit's ability to return to the owner's hand make the DDDD's direct damage spells useless.

Winter Orbs pose a problem for the DDDD, because they make the Fireballs and Disintegrates very difficult to cast effectively. Hand Destruction can also present a problem for the DDDD. If enough Hymns and a Hand Destruction pounce on the DDDD it has trouble recovering.

Deck Name: Forest Fire

Block One	Block Two	Block Three
Pocket 1	Pocket 1	Pocket 1
Mishra's Factory	Elvish Archers	Strip Mine
Mishra's Factory	Elvish Archers	Forest
Mishra's Factory	Elvish Archers	Forest
Mishra's Factory	Elvish Archers	Forest
Pocket 2	Pocket 2	Pocket 2
Nevinyrral's Disk	Fyndhorn Elves	Forest
Nevinyrral's Disk	Fyndhorn Elves	Forest
Nevinyrral's Disk	Joven's Ferrets	Mountain
Feldon's Cane	Joven's Ferrets	Mountain
Pocket 3	Pocket 3	Pocket 3
Lightning Bolt	Ernham Djinn	Mountain
Lightning Bolt	Ernham Djinn	Mountain
Lightning Bolt	Ernham Djinn	Mountain
Lightning Bolt	Ernham Djinn	Karplusan Forest
Pocket 4	Pocket 4	Pocket 4
Incinerate	Autumn Willow	Karplusan Forest
Incinerate	Lhurgoyf	Karplusan Forest
Incinerate	Night Soil	Karplusan Forest
Incinerate	Stunted Growth	Stormbind
Pocket 5	Pocket 5	Pocket 5
Marton Stromgald	Strip Mine	Llanowar Elves
Jayemdae Tome	Strip Mine	Llanowar Elves
Jayemdae Tome	Strip Mine	Llanowar Elves
Zuran Orb	Strip Mine	Llanowar Elves

Sideboard:

1. Hurricane
2. Hurricane
3. Hurricane
4. Birds of Paradise
5. Birds of Paradise
6. Pyroblast
7. Pyroblast
8. Pyroblast
9. Tranquility
10. Tranquility
11. Crumble
12. Crumble
13. Crumble
14. Anarchy
15. Anarchy

Use Hurricanes to stop flyers, Birds of Paradise if an opponent uses Earthquake, Pyroblast to stop Counterspell decks and Control Magic, Tranquilities for enchantment heavy decks, Crumble for artifact heavy decks, and Anarchy for decks with white permanents.

Alvaro Susa, a man with high credentials, sent me this deck. Alvaro is a good friend of Adam Maysonet's, and knowledgeable players in the Miami area recognize him for his playing skill. This deck represents more of a hybrid of many deck types than a pure Disk deck. Forest Fire is a creature deck. It seems Alvaro uses the Disks to control the tempo of the game. The creatures that Alvaro utilizes have a direct connection with the Disk. The Elves frequently quicken the casting of the Disk, while the Lhurgoyf benefits from the activation of the Disk.

Chapter 8:

Tome Decks

"Good Players use the Book"
—Adam Maysonet

The Jayemdae Tome stands as the most powerful artifact in Type II.

Perhaps the most important element in Magic is card economy. That is what the Tome provides. Many players find the Tome's four casting cost and four activation cost too unwieldy to use properly. The players who subscribe to this belief are those addicted to winning in the early game. If you manage to survive the early game (first four turns) and have a Jayemdae Tome in play, it will be a matter of a few turns before it pays for itself by providing you with the mana sources necessary to run it. Once you pounce to a four-card jump on your opponent, chances are that he will not recover and the game will be yours.

Deck Name: The Engine

Block One	Block Two	Block Three
Pocket 1	Pocket 1	Pocket 1
Jayemdae Tome	Fountain of Youth	Zuran Orb
Jayemdae Tome	Fountain of Youth	City of Brass
Jayemdae Tome	Recall	City of Brass

Counterspell	Ivory Tower	Underground River
Pocket 2	Pocket 2	Pocket 2
Counterspell	Zur's Weirding	Adarkar Wastes
Icy Manipulator	Power Sink	Adarkar Wastes
Icy Manipulator	Power Sink	Adarkar Wastes
Icy Manipulator	Power Sink	Adarkar Wastes
Pocket 3	Pocket 3	Pocket 3
Wrath of God	Disenchant	Island
Wrath of God	Disenchant	Island
Wrath of God	Disenchant	Island
Wrath of God	Fireball	Island
Pocket 4	Pocket 4	Pocket 4
Swords to Plowshares	Mishra's Factory	Island
Swords to Plowshares	Mishra's Factory	Plains
Swords to Plowshares	Mishra's Factory	Plains
Balance	Mishra's Factory	Plains
Pocket 5	Pocket 5	Pocket 5
Blinking Spirit	Fellwar Stone	Plains
Blinking Spirit	Fellwar Stone	Plains
Blinking Spirit	Fellwar Stone	Plains
Control Magic	Fellwar Stone	Plains

Sideboard:

1. Sleight of Mind	6. C.O.P. Red	11. Divine Offering
2. C.O.P. Black	7. C.O.P. Red	12. Divine Offering
3. C.O.P. Black	8. C.O.P White	13. Swords to Plowshares
4. C.O.P. Black	9. C.O.P. White	14. Control Magic
5. C.O.P. Red	10. Disenchant	15. Serra Angel

Use the Sleight of Mind as an intimidation tool for black players, C.O.P. Blacks for Black decks, C.O.P. Reds for Red decks, C.O.P. Whites for White decks, Disenchant for Artifact heavy decks, Swords to Plowshares for Hand Destruction decks, Control Magic for Hand Destruction or Creature decks, and Serra Angel for a second game against a non-black player.

When I went to Origins to play for the National Championship, I had the opportunity to play against Chris Pantages, one of the better players from the Bay area of California. When I played Chris, I used a version of my Disk deck. Chris beat me soundly. His deck centered on the Jayemdae Tome. I noticed that Chris was using not one, or even two Jayemdae Tomes, but three. He outdrew me, and I suffered to the superiority of his deck's card economy.

When I returned home to Dallas, my addiction to the Disk continued and I did not immediately convert to the use of the Tome. I persisted with Disks for some time, until I decided to try and construct a Zur's Weirding deck. Originally I started playing with the Jalum Tome, which allowed me to cycle through the deck very quickly. Then I remembered playing against Chris and tried playing with the Jayemdae Tome. The speed at which games turned to my favor once the Tome was in play surprised me. The obvious utility of the Tome motivated me to fashion my own deck, which I dubbed the Engine.

When I constructed the original Engine, I patterned it around the Zur's Weirding. I included the Fountains, Zuran Orb, and Ivory Towers to cut the cost of life for using the Weirding, and thus made its price less disruptive to pay.

Consider the versatility of the Weirding's use. Once you have a Weirding in play and your opponent has no means for dealing damage, the life-providing cards can establish a lock, or at least a partial lock, on the match's control. The life-providing cards offset the Weirding's damage. For example, if you have one Fountain in play, you can deny an opponent one card every two rounds and retain your life total. If, on the other hand, you have two Fountains in play, or an Ivory Tower and six cards in your hand, then you can deny your opponent every card he draws. In another situation, you may have a Weirding and a Zuran Orb and can exchange the two points of damage from the Weirding with a two-point gain from the sacrifice of a land to the Zuran Orb to deny your opponent cards. When the Tomes and a Weirding were in play, the Weirding actually became a damage card. This wonderful transformation occurred because opponents needed to stop me from acquiring the many useful cards, including damage spells, that the deck contains.

The original Engine deck contained two Zur's Weirdings in it, but I reduced them to one because of the many times I suffered the misfortune of drawing both of them in my first hand. Though the Engine started out as a Weirding deck, it eventually trans-formed into a Tome deck. The extra cards that the Tomes allow you to draw provide enough reaction and removal that an opponent can accomplish little or nothing.

When playing the Engine, use the Blinking Spirits with the Wrath of God. You can cast the Wrath of God and return the Spirits to your hand. The Spirits are also extremely durable creatures, making them excellent cards to use with Zur's Weirding. For example, if both players use Zur's Weirding to prevent each other from drawing cards and the Blinking Spirit is in play, the opponent will experience extreme difficulty destroying the Spirit. If he doesn't have a means to block or force you to pick the Spirit back up, he faces a consistent source of damage.

The Icy Manipulators carry multiple uses in the Engine deck. The principal use of the Manipulators is to lock down an opponent's creatures so you can hold your Wrath of God until the last minute. Now you can maximize card economy by killing two or more creatures. The Icys can also tie down an opponent's mana when a Weirding comes into play. Often you can execute this and deny the use of an entire color of an opponent's deck.

This deck plays well overall but manifests one major weakness: Hand Destruction ravages it. Although this deck competes strongly with all of the other deck types, it is inferior against any well cut Hand Destruction deck because it will lose to early Hymn to Touraches, Mindstab Thrulls, and Hypnotic Specters.

Deck Name: Titania's Book

Block One	Block Two	Block Three
Pocket 1	Pocket 1	Pocket 1
Jayemdae Tome	Llanowar Elves	Fellwar Stone
Jayemdae Tome	Llanowar Elves	Fellwar Stone
Jayemdae Tome	Titania's Song	Fellwar Stone
Jayemdae Tome	Titania's Song	Karplusan Forest
Pocket 2	Pocket 2	Pocket 2
Icy Manipulator	Ernham Djinn	Karplusan Forest
Icy Manipulator	Ernham Djinn	Karplusan Forest
Icy Manipulator	Ernham Djinn	Karplusan Forest
Icy Manipulator	Ernham Djinn	City of Brass

Pocket 3	Pocket 3	Pocket 3
Lightning Bolt	Elvish Archer	City of Brass
Lightning Bolt	Elvish Archer	Mountain
Lightning Bolt	Elvish Archer	Mountain
Lightning Bolt	Elvish Archer	Mountain
Pocket 4	Pocket 4	Pocket 4
Incinerate	Mishra's Factory	Mountain
Incinerate	Mishra's Factory	Forest
Incinerate	Mishra's Factory	Forest
Fireball	Mishra's Factory	Forest
Pocket 5	Pocket 5	Pocket 5
Fireball	Sylvan Library	Forest
Fireball	Nature's Lore	Forest
Fireball	Nature's Lore	Forest
Titania's Song	Fellwar Stone	Forest

Sideboard:

1. Lifeforce	6. Whirling Dervish	11. Crumble
2. Lifeforce	7. Shatter	12. Pyroclasym
3. Whirling Dervish	8. Shatter	13. Pyroclasym
4. Whirling Dervish	9. Shatter	14. Pyroblast
5. Whirling Dervish	10. Crumble	15. Pyroblast

Use Lifeforces for Hand Destruction decks, Shatters for Artifact heavy decks, Pyroclasyms for Small Creature decks, and Pyroblast for Blue decks.

This is a version of the Tome deck that is much more active than the Engine deck. This version includes ten creatures that put early pressure on an opponent. The Icys and Tomes first provide the benefits of their special abilities until enough are in play. The next step is to draw a Titania's Song. With the Song in hand and a large number of artifacts in play, you can overrun an opponent with twelve more creatures, twelve more creatures that he is not expecting. Once Titania's Song enters play, this deck's direct damage can eliminate an opponent's artifacts if such a need arises.

Deck Name: Wiseman and Pantages' (W&P) Book Deck

Block One	Block Two	Block Three
Pocket 1	Pocket 1	Pocket 1
Serra Angel	Recall	City of Brass
Serra Angel	Feldon's Cane	City of Brass
Serra Angel	Deflection	City of Brass
Serra Angel	Deflection	Adarkar Wastes
Pocket 2	Pocket 2	Pocket 2
Savanna Lion	Zuran Orb	Strip Mine
Savanna Lion	Jayemdae Tome	Strip Mine
Savanna Lion	Jayemdae Tome	Strip Mine
Savanna Lion	Jayemdae Tome	Strip Mine
Pocket 3	Pocket 3	Pocket 3
Mishra's Factory	Swords to Plowshares	Adarkar Wastes
Mishra's Factory	Swords to Plowshares	Adarkar Wastes
Mishra's Factory	Swords to Plowshares	Adarkar Wastes
Mishra's Factory	Swords to Plowshares	Plains
Pocket 4	Pocket 4	Pocket 4
Fireball	Disenchant	Plains
Fireball	Disenchant	Plains
Fireball	Disenchant	Plains
Fireball	Disenchant	Plains
Pocket 5	Pocket 5	Pocket 5
Lightning Bolt	Jester's Cap	Mountain
Lightning Bolt	Fellwar Stone	Mountain
Lightning Bolt	Fellwar Stone	Mountain
Lightning Bolt	Fellwar Stone	Mountain

Sideboard:

1. Meekstone	6. Divine Offering	11. Land Tax
2. Meekstone	7. Divine Offering	12. Land Tax
3. Meekstone	8. Divine Offering	13. C.O.P. Red
4. Karma	9. Pyroclasym	14. C.O.P. Red
5. Karma	10. Pyroclasym	15. C.O.P. Red

Use the Meekstones for Large Creature decks, Karmas for predominately Black decks, Divine Offerings for heavy artifact decks, Pyroclasyms for Small Fast Creature decks, Land Taxes for Land Destruction and Hand Destruction decks, and C.O.P. Reds for Burn decks.

This is the deck Chris played when we met at Origins. The W&P Book deck is one of the strongest decks I have ever encountered in Type II. The only decks I have seen that can beat it more than fifty percent of the time are the Engine and decks with Gloom. The W&P is probably a better all around deck than the Engine because of its precise use of both active elements and reactive elements. The Engine is too reactive to be a reliable deck in the Swiss style; time constraints are too limiting.

The W&P maintains strength throughout the entire game. In the early game the W&P has the Savanna Lions to pressure an opponent. If an opponent blunders foolishly enough to use a Swords to Plowshares on the Lion, that is a Swords to Plowshares he will not have to remove a Serra Angel. The deck's four Bolts, four Swords to Plowshares, and four Fireballs can handle any early annoyance.

In the mid game, the W&P asserts itself with the power of the Tomes and Angels. Also during the mid game, the Deflections come online and can routinely turn an opponent's game-winning Fireball on themselves. The Deflection, like a Control Magic or a Hymn to Tourach, gives a two for one card advantage over an opponent.

After the deck passes from the mid game to the late game, the Fireballs become increasingly fatal. In some cases the W&P will have two Tomes running at the same time. When the W&P achieves this state, it's an avalanche falling on the opponent.

Deck Name: The Pantages Pummeler

Block One	Block Two	Block Three
Pocket 1	Pocket 1	Pocket 1
Ernham Djinn	Lightning Bolt	Karplusan Forest
Ernham Djinn	Lightning Bolt	City of Brass
Ernham Djinn	Lightning Bolt	City of Brass
Ernham Djinn	Lightning Bolt	City of Brass
Pocket 2	Pocket 2	Pocket 2
Johtull Wurm	Jayemdae Tome	Brushland
Force of Nature	Jayemdae Tome	Plains
Force of Nature	Jayemdae Tome	Plains
Force of Nature	Jayemdae Tome	Plains

Pocket 3	Pocket 3	Pocket 3
Llanowar Elves	Disenchant	Brushland
Llanowar Elves	Disenchant	Mountain
Llanowar Elves	Disenchant	Mountain
Llanowar Elves	Fireball	Mountain
Pocket 4	Pocket 4	Pocket 4
Autumn Willow	Swords to Plowshares	Forest
Autumn Willow	Swords to Plowshares	Forest
Elvish Archers	Fireball	Forest
Elvish Archers	Fellwar Stone	Forest
Pocket 5	Pocket 5	Pocket 5
Stunted Growth	Fellwar Stone	Forest
Stunted Growth	Fellwar Stone	Forest
Stunted Growth	Fellwar Stone	Forest
Zuran Orb	Karplusan Forest	Forest

Sideboard:

1. Lifeforce	6. Swords to Plowshares	11. Pyroclasym
2. Lifeforce	7. Disenchant	12. Fireball
3. Lifeforce	8. Crumble	13. Pyroblast
4. Lifeforce	9. Crumble	14. Pyroblast
5. Swords to Plowshares	10. Pyroclasym	15. Pyroblast

Use the Lifeforces for predominately Black decks, Swords to Plowshares if opponent has few artifacts, Disenchant if opponent has many artifacts, Pyroclasms for Small Fast Creature decks, and Pyroblasts for decks with Control Magic.

This a slightly modified version of a deck sent to me by Chris Pantages. This deck is built around exploiting the somewhat imbalanced green creatures in a mana-rich environment, combined with enough defense to win consistently. It is worth noting that even in this offensive deck, four Tomes in the standard deck speeds up this already fast deck considerably.

One of the more dynamic features of this deck is the Stunted Growth. If you have a creature in play that your opponent cannot deal with and you manage to cast a Stunted Growth, your opponent will suffer to that creature for another three turns before he can eliminate it. This is because he will draw the three cards he had in his hand earlier which could not deal with the creature.

For Those Who Fear the Hymns

Many talented players become discouraged when they lose to amateur players using simple yet effective decks that have been popular for a while. One of the more annoying types of these decks centers on Hand Destruction. Enter the Jayemdae Tome, a natural counter to Hand Destruction decks. This card can fill your hand faster than your opponent can empty it. Steve Fraley and Henry Stern constructed these two Tome decks in response to the Hand Destruction bother.

Deck Name: The Fraley Special

Block One	Block Two	Block Three
Pocket 1	Pocket 1	Pocket 1
Counterspell	Ghost Ship	City of Brass
Counterspell	Ghost Ship	City of Brass
Deflection	Ghost Ship	City of Brass
Deflection	Ghost Ship	Mountain
Pocket 2	Pocket 2	Pocket 2
Disenchant	Eron the Relentless	Mountain
Disenchant	Eron the Relentless	Mountain
Fireball	Mishra's Factory	Mountain
Fireball	Mishra's Factory	Mountain
Pocket 3	Pocket 3	Pocket 3
Lightning Bolt	Jayemdae Tome	Mountain
Lightning Bolt	Jayemdae Tome	Adarkar Wastes
Lightning Bolt	Jayemdae Tome	Adarkar Wastes
Lightning Bolt	Balance	Adarkar Wastes
Pocket 4	Pocket 4	Pocket 4
Incinerate	Barbed Sextant	Adarkar Wastes
Incinerate	Barbed Sextant	Island
Incinerate	Barbed Sextant	Island
Incinerate	Barbed Sextant	Island
Pocket 5	Pocket 5	Pocket 5
Swords to Plowshares	Fellwar Stone	Island
Control Magic	Fellwar Stone	Island

Control Magic	Fellwar Stone	Island
Control Magic	Fellwar Stone	Island

Sideboard:

1. Control Magic	6. Pyroblast	11. Pyroclasym
2. Incinerate	7. Pyroblast	12. Pyroclasym
3. Power Sink	8. Pyroblast	13. Pyroclasym
4. Power Sink	9. Disenchant	14. Hydroblast
5. Pyroblast	10. Disenchant	15. Hydroblast

Use Control Magic for Large Creature decks and Hand Destruction decks, Incinerate for Creature heavy decks, Power Sinks for Hand Destruction decks, Pyroblasts for Blue-based decks, Disenchant for Artifact-based decks, and Hydroblasts for Red-based decks.

Steve Fraley, the "old man" of southern Magic, constructed this deck in response to an increase in Hand Destruction decks that were beginning to accost Dallas-area Magic. Most Hand Destruction decks cannot deal with either Ghost Ships or Control Magics. A Ghost Ship can block any creature a Hand Destruction deck can put into play, making it the optimal card to stop the Creature Hand Destruction. Steve's use of Barbed Sextants in conjunction with his Cities of Brass furnishes his deck the necessary mana to run four colors.

Deck Name: Henry Stern's (2nd at Nationals, 3rd at World) White/Green Tome

Block One	Block Two	Block Three
Pocket 1	Pocket 1	Pocket 1
Llanowar Elves	Savanna Lions	Fellwar Stone
Llanowar Elves	Savanna Lions	Fellwar Stone
Llanowar Elves	Savanna Lions	Brushland
Llanowar Elves	Savanna Lions	Brushland
Pocket 2	Pocket 2	Pocket 2
Whirling Dervish	Balance	Brushland
Whirling Dervish	Zuran Orb	Brushland
Whirling Dervish	Swords to Plowshares	Plains
Whirling Dervish	Swords to Plowshares	Plains
Pocket 3	Pocket 3	Pocket 3

Ernham Djinn	Swords to Plowshares	Plains
Ernham Djinn	Swords to Plowshares	Plains
Ernham Djinn	Disenchant	Plains
Ernham Djinn	Disenchant	Plains
Pocket 4	Pocket 4	Pocket 4
Lhurgoyf	Disenchant	Plains
Lhurgoyf	Disenchant	Forest
Serra Angel	Mishra's Factory	Forest
Serra Angel	Mishra's Factory	Forest
Pocket 5	Pocket 5	Pocket 5
Serra Angel	Mishra's Factory	Forest
Jayemdae Tome	Mishra's Factory	Forest
Jayemdae Tome	Fellwar Stone	Forest
Jayemdae Tome	Fellwar Stone	Forest

Sideboard:

1. C.O.P. Red	6. C.O.P. Black	11. C.O.P. Green
2. C.O.P. Red	7. Karma	12. C.O.P. Green
3. C.O.P. Red	8. Karma	13. Jayemdae Tome
4. C.O.P. Black	9. Divine Offering	14. Autumn Willow
5. C.O.P. Black	10. Divine Offering	15. Lhurgoyf

Use C.O.P. Red and Autumn Willow for Burn decks, C.O.P. Black for Black decks, Divine Offering for Artifact decks, C.O.P. Green for Green decks, and Jayemdae Tome for Hand Destruction decks.

Henry built this deck to combat a number of straight red and straight black decks that had been popping up around the Los Angeles area. The large quantity of creatures in this deck puts a Burn deck on the run. The three Tomes and four Whirling Dervishes are enough to overcome ninety-five percent of the black Hand Destruction decks. Though this is a deck built to compete in the Metagame, Henry has made it generally competitive.

Tome decks are not as complicated as Disk decks. Most of the Tome decks depend on cards that are independently useful. If you have to trade your cards one for one, then it follows that if you draw more cards than your opponent, you will win. Because each card in a Tome deck is independently powerful, these decks are harder to overcome. One cannot simply smash a link and break the chain.

Chapter 9:

Millstone Decks

Millstone decks stand as the most passive and reactive type of decks in Magic. Millstone decks function on the strategy of achieving victory by grinding up your opponent's cards. Millstones cause your opponent to discard two cards from his library for a cost of two mana. Many players thrive on the Millstone deck's unusual road to victory because the deck effectively destroys the utility of many of an opponent's cards. Most Millstone decks inflict no damage, thus all life-giving cards like Reverse Damage, Zuran Orb, Fountain of

---

Cards That Work Well in Millstone Decks

Artifacts
1. Feldon's Cane
2. Fountain of Youth
3. Howling Mine
4. Ivory Tower
5. Millstone
6. Sunstone
7. Zuran Orb

White
1. Balance
2. Island Sanctuary
3. Prophecy
4. Swords to
   Plowshares
5. Wrath of God

Blue
1. Counterspell
2. Memory Lapse
3. Merchant Scroll
4. Mystic Decree
5. Portent
6. Power Sink
7. Ray of Erasure
8. Recall
9. Reef Pirates
10. Spell Blast
11. Zur's Weirding

Red
1. Orcish Spy

Land
1. Glacial Chasm
2. Ice Floe

Youth, and Ivory Tower are completely useless. Also, cards that provide protection like Circles of Protection serve no purpose. Most Millstone decks have no creatures, and so all non-damaging creature removal cards like Wrath of God, Swords to Plowshares, Dark Banishing, and Terror are useless. Because of the deck's unique method for achieving victory, these decks can be very effective.

Deck Name: Lee's Millstone Deck

Block One	Block Two	Block Three
Pocket 1	Pocket 1	Pocket 1
Disenchant	Disenchant	Barbed Sextant
Memory Lapse	Feldon's Cane	Barbed Sextant
Memory Lapse	Spell Blast	Adarkar Wastes
Memory Lapse	Power Sink	Adarkar Wastes
Pocket 2	Pocket 2	Pocket 2
Counterspell	Swords to Plowshares	Adarkar Wastes
Counterspell	Swords to Plowshares	Adarkar Wastes
Counterspell	Swords to Plowshares	City of Brass
Counterspell	Swords to Plowshares	City of Brass
Pocket 3	Pocket 3	Pocket 3
Millstone	Wrath of God	Plains
Millstone	Wrath of God	Plains
Millstone	Wrath of God	Island
Millstone	Ivory Tower	Island
Pocket 4	Pocket 4	Pocket 4
Howling Mine	Island Sanctuary	Island
Howling Mine	Island Sanctuary	Island
Howling Mine	Island Sanctuary	Island
Howling Mine	Zuran Orb	Island
Pocket 5	Pocket 5	Pocket 5
Portent	Recall	Island
Portent	Balance	Island
Portent	Barbed Sextant	Island
Portent	Barbed Sextant	Island

Sideboard:

1. C.O.P. Red	6. C.O.P. White	11. Wrath of God
2. C.O.P. Red	7. C.O.P. White	12. Disenchant
3. C.O.P. Red	8. C.O.P. Black	13. Disenchant
4. C.O.P. Green	9. C.O.P. Black	14. Divine Offering
5. C.O.P. White	10. C.O.P. Black	15. Divine Offering

Use the C.O.P. Reds for Red decks, the C.O.P. Green for Green decks, C.O.P. White for White decks, C.O.P. Blacks for Black decks, Wrath of God for Creature decks, and Disenchants for Artifact intensive decks.

As soon as Homelands hit the shelf, my good friend Lee Abramson constructed a new Millstone deck. When the set came out both Lee and I agreed that the Memory Lapse belonged in Millstone decks. A player can cast a Memory Lapse on an opponent's spell and force him to return it to the top of his deck. Then you can use the Millstone to toss it in the graveyard.

Common Millstone themes run through Lee's deck. The first is the Howling Mine, Island Sanctuary combination. This combination makes the controller impervious to all non-islandwalking, non-flying creatures and still allows him the benefit of drawing a card. The Howling Mines help the Millstone deck with its most plaguing problem: speed. Millstone decks are slow, and because of their slowness, they lose in the Swiss-style tournaments.

Another feature of Lee's deck is the Portent/Millstone combination. The Portent assists this deck, helping you to find a much needed card or eliminating threats in an opponent's deck before he ever draws them. One method for doing this is to cast a Portent on him during your turn. If he verges on drawing a card that could be a threat, you can arrange it as the second or third card and allow him to draw a harmless card. After he draws the harmless card, you can Millstone away the threat.

One of the nicer features of Millstone decks is that your opponent's life total means nothing. Because of this, Swords to Plowshares is an exceptionally formidable card in this deck type. It allows you to remove a creature, no matter how large, for one mana and you suffer no penalty.

Lee played this deck against me many times, and we discovered it works well against many Tier One decks. Its greatest problem arises in Tier Two decks like Hand Destruction and White Weenie, which torture it for its lethargy. Because of these recognized weaknesses and the prevalence of Tier Two decks in many tournaments, Lee has not yet ventured to experiment with this deck in tournament play.

Deck Name: The Chasm and the Stone

Block One	Block Two	Block Three
Pocket 1	Pocket 1	Pocket 1
Glacial Chasm	Wrath of God	City of Brass
Glacial Chasm	Wrath of God	City of Brass
Glacial Chasm	Wrath of God	Adarkar Wastes
Recall	Fountain of Youth	Adarkar Wastes
Pocket 2	Pocket 2	Pocket 2
Millstone	Disenchant	Adarkar Wastes
Millstone	Disenchant	Adarkar Wastes
Millstone	Disenchant	Plains
Millstone	Fountain of Youth	Plains
Pocket 3	Pocket 3	Pocket 3
Howling Mine	Swords to Plowshares	Plains
Howling Mine	Swords to Plowshares	Plains
Howling Mine	Swords to Plowshares	Plains
Howling Mine	Ivory Tower	Plains
Pocket 4	Pocket 4	Pocket 4
Icy Manipulator	Fellwar Stone	Island
Icy Manipulator	Fellwar Stone	Island
Zuran Orb	Fellwar Stone	Island
Balance	Fellwar Stone	Island
Pocket 5	Pocket 5	Pocket 5
Counterspell	Barbed Sextant	Island
Counterspell	Barbed Sextant	Island
Counterspell	Barbed Sextant	Island
Counterspell	Barbed Sextant	Island

Sideboard:

1. C.O.P. Red	6. C.O.P. White	11. Wrath of God
2. C.O.P. Red	7. C.O.P. Black	12. Disenchant
3. C.O.P. Red	8. C.O.P. Black	13. Divine Offering
4. C.O.P. Red	9. Sleight of Mind	14. Divine Offering
5. C.O.P. White	10. Sleight of Mind	15. Divine Offering

This deck resembles Lee's, but it adds the Glacial Chasm. The Chasm prevents creatures from dealing damage for the cumulative upkeep of two life. This is valuable. The Chasm can give you three turns of undisturbed Millstone use. If, for instance, you have a Howling Mine in play with two Millstones, the Chasm can grind six cards per turn off your opponent's library. Over three turns, for a cost of six life, you can grind off eighteen cards. That figure is almost a third of a standard size deck. If a Chasm is in play and you wish to sidestep its upkeep cost, you can sacrifice it to the Zuran Orb and replace two of those lost points of life. Of course, you can opt not to pay the upkeep cost and sacrifice it to your graveyard, but with the Orb you increase the Chasm's benefit.

This version of the Millstone deck has Icy Manipulators in it, which allow you to lock down an opponent's creature, no matter how large or threatening, until he casts a second one. Once a second creature enters into play, you can then cast your Wrath of God and enjoy two-for-one card count economy. After casting the Wrath, the Icy will lock down the next creature your opponent puts into play.

Deck Name: The Weirding Stone

Block One	Block Two	Block Three
Pocket 1	Pocket 1	Pocket 1
Millstone	Zur's Weirding	City of Brass
Millstone	Zur's Weirding	Adarkar Wastes
Millstone	Ivory Tower	Adarkar Wastes
Millstone	Fountain of Youth	Adarkar Wastes
Pocket 2	Pocket 2	Pocket 2
Counterspell	Wrath of God	Adarkar Wastes
Counterspell	Wrath of God	Plains
Counterspell	Wrath of God	Plains

Counterspell	Wrath of God	Plains
Pocket 3	Pocket 3	Pocket 3
Icy Manipulator	Balance	Plains
Icy Manipulator	Spell Blast	Plains
Icy Manipulator	Recall	Plains
Fountain of Youth	Zuran Orb	Island
Pocket 4	Pocket 4	Pocket 4
Disenchant	Disrupting Scepter	Island
Disenchant	Feldon's Cane	Island
Disenchant	Fellwar Stone	Island
Disrupting Scepter	Fellwar Stone	Island
Pocket 5	Pocket 5	Pocket 5
Power Sink	Fellwar Stone	Island
Power Sink	Fellwar Stone	Island
Power Sink	City of Brass	Island
Power Sink	City of Brass	Island

Sideboard:

1. C.O.P. Red	6. Hydroblast	11. Disenchant
2. C.O.P. Red	7. Howling Mine	12. Divine Offering
3. C.O.P. Red	8. Howling Mine	13. Divine Offering
4. Hydroblast	9. Howling Mine	14. Serra Angel
5. Hydroblast	10. Howling Mine	15. Serra Angel

Use the C.O.P. Reds for Burn decks, Hydroblasts for Red decks, Howling Mines for Hand Destruction decks, Disenchant for Artifact intensive decks, and Serra Angels for the Transformational nuisances.

Deck Name: The Spy Deck

Block One	Block Two	Block Three
Pocket 1	Pocket 1	Pocket 1
Orcish Spy	Savanna Lions	Mountain
Orcish Spy	Savanna Lions	Mountain
Orcish Spy	Savanna Lions	Mountain
Orcish Spy	Savanna Lions	Mountain
Pocket 2	Pocket 2	Pocket 2
Lightning Bolt	Howling Mine	Mountain

Lightning Bolt	Howling Mine	Mountain
Lightning Bolt	Howling Mine	Mountain
Lightning Bolt	Howling Mine	Mountain
Pocket 3	Pocket 3	Pocket 3
Incinerate	Spirit Link	City of Brass
Incinerate	Spirit Link	City of Brass
Incinerate	Balance	Plains
Incinerate	Disenchant	Plains
Pocket 4	Pocket 4	Pocket 4
Swords to Plowshares	Millstone	Plains
Swords to Plowshares	Millstone	Plains
Swords to Plowshares	Millstone	Plains
Swords to Plowshares	Disenchant	Plains
Pocket 5	Pocket 5	Pocket 5
Primordial Ooze	Serra Angel	Plains
Primordial Ooze	Serra Angel	Plains
Primordial Ooze	Fireball	Plains
Primordial Ooze	Fireball	Plains

Sideboard:

1. Disenchant	6. C.O.P. Red	11. Millstone
2. Disenchant	7. C.O.P. Red	12. Wrath of God
3. Divine Offering	8. C.O.P. Red	13. Wrath of God
4. Divine Offering	9. Fireball	14. Spirit Link
5. Divine Offering	10. Fireball	15. Spirit Link

Use Disenchants for Artifact decks, C.O.P. Reds for Red decks, and Fireballs for Transformational decks.

This Millstone deck epitomizes transformational deck theory. During the first game, the Millstones act as a secondary theme with the Orcish Spies. You can tap a Spy and view your opponent's top three cards, then Millstone away any threats that you observe. These two cards are for control rather than a road to victory.

An opponent must deal with the early pressure of the Primordial Ooze, Orcish Spies, and Savanna Lions. With twelve instant creature removals (Swords, Bolts, Incinerates) to support creatures, you can frequently win a match by overwhelming an opponent in the early game. In some cases, the Ooze becomes too troublesome to keep around. You have several ways to dispose of it in this deck. For example, you can Swords to Plowshares it, or Spirit Link it to avoid its upkeep costs.

In the second game, an opponent may sideboard in his Circle of Protection: Red to render the Ooze and Burn damage useless. This is when you can switch out a majority of your active cards for the reactive cards that make deck depletion the primary goal of the deck. You can add more burn spells for creature removal and take out many of your own creatures. This should prove difficult for an opponent to manage. The Spy deck has the potential for twenty-two anti-creature spells, making it virtually impossible to overrun.

Problems with Millstone Decks

Typically, Millstone decks are slow, making them poor choices for Swiss style tournaments. As discussed before, Swiss-style tournaments operate with timed matches. If it takes you a long period of time to grind down an opponent, you may not finish some games. This implies that you will lose points, and your overall tournament rating will not rank high enough for qualification in the semifinals.

Chapter 10:

Power Surge and Manabarbs Decks

Cards That Work Well in Power Surge Decks

Red
1. Detonate
2. Disintegrate
3. Dwarven Catapult
4. Power Surge
5. Fireball
6. Incinerate
7. Lava Burst
8. Lightning Bolt
9. Power Surge
10. Shivan Dragon

Black
1. Drain Life
2. Hymn to Tourach
3. Hypnotic Specter
4. Initiates of the Ebon Hand
5. Mind Ravel
6. Mind Warp
7. Mindstab Thrull
8. Order of the Ebon Hand
9. Soul Burn

Green
1. Stunted Growth
2. Tranquility

Blue
1. Ice Floe
2. Time Elemental

White
1. Blinking Spirit
2. Icatian Infantry

Artifacts
1. Disrupting Scepter
2. Jayemdae Tome
3. Sunglasses of Urza

Land
1. Glacial Chasm
2. Mishra's Factory

Both the Power Surges and Manabarbs qualify as some of the most powerful cards in Magic. Though they both bear weaknesses, used properly their effect can devastate opposing decks. However, there are nuances to these cards that players should have a firm grasp on. Both the Power Surge and the Manabarbs create an environment in which both duelists must proceed with turns cautiously. Any realistic player must know how to protect himself in such an environment.

Power Surge Decks

Power Surge is one of those cards that will either win you the game or prove totally useless. There are some Tier One decks constructed around the Power Surge. One advantage of the Power Surge is that, as an enchantment, it can act as a constant source of damage.

The Power Surge waxes and wanes in popularity. This card is extremely particular in usage. It shows immense power in some instances and utter worthlessness in others. In the early game, the Power Surge is often useless. An opponent is more likely to sustain damage from the Surge in the mid or late game, when he has a large amount of land and fewer cards in hand to cast. In the late game the Surge may win the game for you, given your opponent has no Mishra's Factories, Icatian Infantry, or C.O.P. Red.

Problems with the Power Surge

Most experienced players know that both the Factories and the Infantry can serve as mana sinks to avoid Surge damage. The reason for this is a player can activate his special ability over and over again in response to each previous activation. Many Power Surge players use this capability to their own advantage so that they avoid the Surge. A method to deny an opponent this same advantage is to stock a large amount of creature removal to prevent the opportunity to use a mana dump.

Another problem for Power Surge decks arises in Circle of Protection Red. Power Surge decks must consist of some form of enchantment removal. The best cards to use for this are Disenchant, Desert Twister, and Arenson's Aura, all of which can destroy a Circle of Protection without destroying all the enchantments, like a Tranquility or Disk will. There is one other route a Power Surge deck user can try. He can use Ghostly Flame, which makes damage from red and black spells colorless, to escape the Circles. But if your opponent uses Circles, then he probably uses Disenchant as well.

Observe also that the Power Surge is redundant. If you have two in play, an opponent can mana burn himself at the end of your turn to avoid taking the doubled Power Surge damage. If they are thoughtful players, they will take an equivalent amount of damage whether you have one or two Power Surges in play.

Deck Name: Red's Surge Deck

Block One	Block Two	Block Three
Pocket 1	Pocket 1	Pocket 1
Power Surge	Fireball	Mishra's Factory
Power Surge	Fireball	Mishra's Factory
Power Surge	Fireball	City of Brass
Swords to Plowshares	Fireball	City of Brass
Pocket 2	Pocket 2	Pocket 2
Disrupting Scepter	Disenchant	Mountain
Disrupting Scepter	Disenchant	Mountain
Disrupting Scepter	Disenchant	Mountain
Swords to Plowshares	Zuran Orb	Mountain
Pocket 3	Pocket 3	Pocket 3
Blinking Spirit	Serra Angel	Mountain
Blinking Spirit	Serra Angel	Mountain
Blinking Spirit	Barbed Sextant	Mountain
Swords to Plowshares	Barbed Sextant	Mountain
Pocket 4	Pocket 4	Pocket 4
Rack	Barbed Sextant	Plains
Rack	Barbed Sextant	Plains
Rack	Fellwar Stone	Plains
Rack	Fellwar Stone	Plains

Pocket 5	Pocket 5	Pocket 5
Lightning Bolt	Fellwar Stone	Plains
Lightning Bolt	Fellwar Stone	Plains
Lightning Bolt	Mishra's Factory	Plains
Lightning Bolt	Mishra's Factory	Plains

Sideboard:

1. C.O.P. Red	6. C.O.P. White	11. Karma
2. C.O.P. Red	7. C.O.P. White	12. Karma
3. C.O.P. Red	8. Pyroclasym	13. Disenchant
4. Jester's Cap	9. Pyroclasym	14. Divine Offering
5. C.O.P. White	10. Pyroclasym	15. Divine Offering

Use C.O.P. Reds for Red decks, Jester's Cap to remove opponent's C.O.P. Red or Blinking Spirits, C.O.P. Whites for White decks, Pyroclasyms for Small Creature decks, Karmas for Black decks, and Disenchant for artifact intensive decks.

This was one of Red's (Brian Sammon) first attempts at a Type II deck. Originally, he used four Power Surges, four Disrupting Scepters, and four Uthden Trolls. As time progressed, Red dropped the Trolls and added Blinking Spirits. Spirits are optimal in Power Surge decks. They not only serve as unremovable creatures, but they can assist as a sink for your mana. Accomplish this by returning the Spirit to your hand multiple times and recasting it until you expend all the excess mana. The best time to do this is after the attack phase. This will allow you to maximize the use of your Spirit.

The Spirits are not the only mana dump in this deck. Red also includes the Mishra's Factories and the Disrupting Scepters. The Scepters enable you to empty your opponent's hand, forcing him to suffer to both the Rack and the Power Surge. If your opponent's hand is empty, each turn he draws a land and he is unable to tap his mana, the Power Surge will pound him for more precious life. The effect of this is similar to that of an all-black player facing a Karma. Other more obvious mana sinks are red X spells.

Deck Name: The Song and Surge

Block One	Block Two	Block Three
Pocket 1	Pocket 1	Pocket 1
Power Surge	Nevinyrral's Disk	Sulfurous Springs
Power Surge	Nevinyrral's Disk	Sulfurous Springs
Power Surge	Nevinyrral's Disk	Sulfurous Springs
Mana Flare	Vampire	Sulfurous Springs
Pocket 2	Pocket 2	Pocket 2
Hymn to Tourach	Mishra's Factory	City of Brass
Hymn to Tourach	Mishra's Factory	City of Brass
Hymn to Tourach	Mishra's Factory	City of Brass
Hymn to Tourach	Mishra's Factory	Mountain
Pocket 3	Pocket 3	Pocket 3
Rack	Fireball	Mountain
Rack	Fireball	Mountain
Rack	Fireball	Mountain
Rack	Fireball	Mountain
Pocket 4	Pocket 4	Pocket 4
Lightning Bolt	Disintegrate	Swamp
Lightning Bolt	Disrupting Scepter	Swamp
Lightning Bolt	Disrupting Scepter	Swamp
Lightning Bolt	Disrupting Scepter	Swamp
Pocket 5	Pocket 5	Pocket 5
Incinerate	Barbed Sextant	Swamp
Incinerate	Barbed Sextant	Swamp
Vampire	Barbed Sextant	Swamp
Balance	Barbed Sextant	Swamp

Sideboard:

1. Tranquility
2. Tranquility
3. Disenchant
4. Shatter
5. Shatter
6. Detonate
7. Detonate
8. Incinerate
9. Incinerate
10. Dark Banishing
11. Dark Banishing
12. Jester's Cap
13. Pyroblast
14. Pyroblast
15. Pyroblast

Use Tranquilities to counter Circles, Shatters to counter artifacts, Incinerates to counter creatures, Jester's Cap for Blinkers, Circles, and Disenchants, and Pyroblasts for mass small creature removal.

This deck is less complicated and more direct than Red's Power Surge deck, taking a more active strategy by removing cards from your opponent's hand and forcing him to burn under the Power Surge. The Vampires coerce an opponent to deal with them under nuisance theory. They also add another road to victory, that of pure damage, bequeathing more versatility to the deck.

Manabarbs Decks

Many times, Manabarbs decks deal more damage than Power Surge decks. This occurs because there are very few ways to avoid taking Manabarbs damage. When one Manabarbs is in play, players hesitate to tap their lands to cast their spells. When two Manabarbs are in play, players stop tapping their land altogether.

Cards That Work Well in Manabarbs Decks

Artifacts
1. Ankh of Mishra
2. Black Vise
3. Fellwar Stone
4. Howling Mine
5. Ivory Tower
6. Zuran Orb

Land
1. Glacial Chasm
2. Ice Floe

Red
1. Incinerate
2. Lightning Bolt
3. Manabarbs
4. Orcish Lumberjack

Green
1. Birds of Paradise
2. Fyndhorn Elder
3. Fyndhorn Elves
4. Living Artifact
5. Llanowar Elves

Blue
1. Drain Power
2. Iceberg
3. Power Sink

Black
1. Gloom
2. Paralyze
3. Seizures

White
1. Brainwash
2. Island Sancturay

Deck Name: Barbs 'n Stuff

Block One	Block Two	Block Three
Pocket 1	Pocket 1	Pocket 1
Manabarbs	Elvish Archers	Swords to Plowshares
Manabarbs	Elvish Archers	Swords to Plowshares
Manabarbs	Elvish Archers	Giant Growth
Manabarbs	Elvish Archers	Giant Growth
Pocket 2	Pocket 2	Pocket 2
Scryb Sprite	Lightning Bolt	Karplusan Forest
Scryb Sprite	Lightning Bolt	Karplusan Forest
Scryb Sprite	Lightning Bolt	Karplusan Forest
Scryb Sprite	Lightning Bolt	Karplusan Forest
Pocket 3	Pocket 3	Pocket 3
Black Vise	Incinerate	Brushland
Giant Growth	Incinerate	Brushland
Giant Growth	Incinerate	Brushland
Giant Growth	Incinerate	Mountain
Pocket 4	Pocket 4	Pocket 4
Birds of Paradise	Fellwar Stone	Mountain
Birds of Paradise	Fellwar Stone	Mountain
Birds of Paradise	Fellwar Stone	Mountain
Birds of Paradise	Fellwar Stone	Forest
Pocket 5	Pocket 5	Pocket 5
Llanowar Elves	Ernham Djinn	Forest
Llanowar Elves	Ernham Djinn	Forest
Llanowar Elves	Ernham Djinn	Forest
Llanowar Elves	Ernham Djinn	Forest

Sideboard:

1. Shatter
2. Disenchant
3. Disenchant
4. Crumble
5. Crumble
6. Mudslide
7. Mudslide
8. Mudslide
9. Mudslide
10. Pyroblast
11. Pyroblast
12. Pyroblast
13. Fireball
14. Fireball
15. Fireball

Use Shatter for Artifact intensive decks, Mudslides and Fireballs for Creature decks, and Pyroblasts for Blue decks.

This red/green deck exemplifies the most common form of Manabarbs decks. The idea of the deck is to apply early pressure with the small creatures. Then, once a Manabarbs enters play, the deck's controller torments his opponent, forcing him to decide between casting spells and taking damage from the Manabarbs. These decks compete well against many decks, but suffer to others. The Barbs 'n Stuff deck dominates in the early and mid game, and if the deck works successfully, there is little chance that a match will ever reach the late game.

This deck's kryptonite is White Weenie Creature decks. Such a match-up commonly results in too many creatures for the Barbs n' Stuff deck to handle. If Mudslide joins the regular Barbs 'n Stuff deck, the small creature threat diminishes significantly. The pendulum now swings on who has the better draw.

Another major threat to a Manabarbs deck is cards that eliminate its alternate sources of mana. The Barbs 'n Stuff deck uses many of its creatures to produce mana so it can avoid Barb damage it would suffer from its land. If an opponent casts a Pyroclasym, he can eliminate a number of Elves and Birds of Paradise. Such cards cause the Manabarbs deck to suffer poor card economy. Though this deck's effectiveness lapses with many Burn decks and White Weenie Creature decks, it executes exceptionally well against many Tier One decks.

Deck Name: Edamreven's Stormbind Manabarbs Deck

Block One	Block Two	Block Three
Pocket 1	Pocket 1	Pocket 1
Manabarbs	Zuran Orb	Ankh of Mishra
Manabarbs	Stormbind	Ankh of Mishra
Manabarbs	Stormbind	Ankh of Mishra
Manabarbs	Stormbind	Ankh of Mishra
Pocket 2	Pocket 2	Pocket 2
Black Vise	Fyndhorn Elves	City of Brass
Whirling Dervish	Fyndhorn Elves	City of Brass
Whirling Dervish	Fyndhorn Elves	City of Brass
Whirling Dervish	Fyndhorn Elves	Mountain

Pocket 3	Pocket 3	Pocket 3
Howling Mine	Birds of Paradise	Karplusan Forest
Howling Mine	Birds of Paradise	Karplusan Forest
Howling Mine	Birds of Paradise	Karplusan Forest
Howling Mine	Birds of Paradise	Karplusan Forest
Pocket 4	Pocket 4	Pocket 4
Lightning Bolt	Llanowar Elves	Mountain
Lightning Bolt	Llanowar Elves	Mountain
Lightning Bolt	Llanowar Elves	Forest
Lightning Bolt	Llanowar Elves	Forest
Pocket 5	Pocket 5	Pocket 5
Incinerate	Fellwar Stone	Forest
Incinerate	Fellwar Stone	Forest
Incinerate	Fellwar Stone	Forest
Incinerate	Fellwar Stone	Forest

Sideboard:

1. Pyroblast	6. Crumble	11. Shatter
2. Pyroblast	7. Crumble	12. Mudslide
3. Pyroblast	8. Shatter	13. Mudslide
4. Pyroblast	9. Shatter	14. Mudslide
5. Crumble	10. Shatter	15. Mudslide

Use Pyroblasts for Blue decks, Crumbles for Artifact based decks, and Mudslides for Creature decks.

This version of the Manabarbs deck attempts to prevent an opponent from casting permanents. This version contains a great deal more creature mana. This should allow the controller of this deck to hold back some creature mana sources, in case they lose those that are in play. This version of the deck functions better against Creature decks because the Stormbinds provide a constant source of targetable damage. The Stormbinds also terminate the redundancy of unneeded land and extra Stormbinds.

Deck Name: The Chasm Deck

Block One	Block Two	Block Three
Pocket 1	Pocket 1	Pocket 1
Manabarbs	Lightning Bolt	Autumn Willow
Manabarbs	Lightning Bolt	Autumn Willow
Manabarbs	Lightning Bolt	City of Brass
Manabarbs	Lightning Bolt	City of Brass
Pocket 2	Pocket 2	Pocket 2
Black Vise	Fyndhorn Elves	Karplusan Forest
Incinerate	Fyndhorn Elves	Karplusan Forest
Incinerate	Fyndhorn Elves	Karplusan Forest
Giant Growth	Fyndhorn Elves	Karplusan Forest
Pocket 3	Pocket 3	Pocket 3
Llanowar Elves	Fireball	Mountain
Llanowar Elves	Fireball	Mountain
Llanowar Elves	Fireball	Mountain
Llanowar Elves	Sylvan Library	Mountain
Pocket 4	Pocket 4	Pocket 4
Elvish Archers	Glacial Chasm	Forest
Elvish Archers	Glacial Chasm	Forest
Elvish Archers	Glacial Chasm	Forest
Elvish Archers	Zuran Orb	Ashnod's Altar
Pocket 5	Pocket 5	Pocket 5
Birds of Paradise	Fellwar Stone	Forest
Birds of Paradise	Fellwar Stone	Forest
Birds of Paradise	Fellwar Stone	Forest
Birds of Paradise	Fellwar Stone	Forest

Sideboard:

1. Earthquake	6. Shatter	11. Lifeforce
2. Earthquake	7. Crumble	12. Whirling Dervish
3. Earthquake	8. Crumble	13. Whirling Dervish
4. Earthquake	9. Crumble	14. Whirling Dervish
5. Shatter	10. Lifeforce	15. Whirling Dervish

Use Earthquakes for Weenie Creature decks, Shatters for Artifact decks, and Lifeforce for Black decks.

The Glacial Chasm is the keystone of this deck. The idea behind this deck is to place pressure early on with the Vise and the Manabarbs. Most of the time, the Bolts and Incinerates are used for creature control. As turns pass, your land and mana sources should accumulate. When you reach a state where you can either eliminate your opponent with a Fireball or cast an Autumn Willow, then you drop a Glacial Chasm. When the Chasm hits the table, you can tap all the mana you want for that turn without suffering any damage. Often you will find it beneficial to suffer the first two points of damage when your next upkeep comes around. This will supply you two turns in which your opponent cannot attack you and you can cast anything you want. Another recipe for a massive Fireball is to sacrifice creatures to the Altar to provide enough mana to engulf your opponent's skull in flames.

This deck is fun to play, but it is not without its faults. To begin with, drawing the Chasms on the first turn is beyond annoying. Pyroclasm also massacres the weenie creatures it contains. However, this deck has the potential to function well throughout the early (Elvish Archers), middle (Manabarbs), and late game (Autumn Willow, Fireball, Glacial Chasm).

Author's Note

The power of the Manabarbs deck deteriorated severely when the Duelist Convocation restricted the Black Vise. These decks are usually only Tier Two decks, and they do not perform as well as when players could utilize four Black Vises. It is a rare occasion to see a player make it to the finals with a Manabarbs in his deck.

Chapter 11:

Zur's Weirding Decks

Zur's Weirding is, perhaps, the most unique and game altering card to emerge out of the Ice Age expansion. When the Weirding enters play, the game itself changes. With its casting, life becomes a precious resource. If the Weirding comes into play unimpeded, both players must determine a strategy for the rest of the game. In some cases, it may be in your best interest to keep an opponent from maintaining a certain color of available mana. In other cases, you may want to stop him from drawing any creature removal. This analysis depends on the situation.

Usually, the best time to put the Weirding into play is when you have dominance or when you believe that you can achieve dominance. In many cases, when the Weirding comes into play it is easy to predetermine who will win the game. When you have some way to either gain life or remove it from your opponent, and your opponent does not possess such a resource, then you are in the best position to take the game.

Deck Name: Red's Weirding

Block One	Block Two	Block Three
Pocket 1	Pocket 1	Pocket 1
Disrupting Scepter	Zur's Weirding	Fellwar Stone
Disrupting Scepter	Zur's Weirding	Fellwar Stone

Disrupting Scepter	Power Sink	City of Brass
Feldon's Cane	Power Sink	City of Brass
Pocket 2	Pocket 2	Pocket 2
Rack	Disenchant	City of Brass
Rack	Disenchant	Adarkar Wastes
Rack	Disenchant	Adarkar Wastes
Recall	Ivory Tower	Adarkar Wastes
Pocket 3	Pocket 3	Pocket 3
Blinking Spirit	Fountain of Youth	Adarkar Wastes
Blinking Spirit	Fountain of Youth	Plains
Blinking Spirit	Zuran Orb	Plains
Balance	Counterspell	Plains
Pocket 4	Pocket 4	Pocket 4
Wrath of God	Counterspell	Plains
Wrath of God	Counterspell	Plains
Wrath of God	Mishra's Factory	Island
Wrath of God	Mishra's Factory	Island
Pocket 5	Pocket 5	Pocket 5
Swords to Plowshares	Mishra's Factory	Island
Swords to Plowshares	Mishra's Factory	Island
Swords to Plowshares	Fellwar Stone	Island
Swords to Plowshares	Fellwar Stone	Island

Sideboard:

1. Divine Offering
2. Divine Offering
3. Divine Offering
4. Disenchant
5. C.O.P. Red
6. C.O.P. Red
7. C.O.P. Red
8. C.O.P. Black
9. C.O.P. Black
10. C.O.P. White
11. C.O.P. White
12. C.O.P. White
13. Serra Angel
14. Serra Angel
15. Serra Angel

Use the Divine Offerings for Artifact decks, C.O.P. Reds for Red decks, C.O.P. Black for Black decks, C.O.P. Whites for White decks, and Serra Angels for Transformational decks.

Red (Brian Sammon) constructed this deck to play in a series of Swiss-style Mox tournaments at Dallas' own Game Chest. Red modeled his deck after a prototype of the Engine. From there it managed to assume its own form. In play testing, the deck had a lackluster performance against Fast Creature decks (particularly

White Weenie) in the mid and late game. This was mainly because Red's deck owned no Tomes to continually provide him with the reaction capability to overcome his opponent. However, Red's deck possessed the capability to deny his opponent several cards with both the Weirding and the Disrupting Scepters. This made the Racks exceptionally disagreeable for the opponent.

Deck Name: The Weird Hippy Shakes

Block One	Block Two	Block Three
Pocket 1	Pocket 1	Pocket 1
Hypnotic Specter	Zuran Orb	Sulfurous Springs
Hypnotic Specter	Zur's Weirding	Sulfurous Springs
Hypnotic Specter	Zur's Weirding	Sulfurous Springs
Hypnotic Specter	Disrupting Scepter	Sulfurous Springs
Pocket 2	Pocket 2	Pocket 2
Ashen Ghoul	Hymn to Tourach	City of Brass
Ashen Ghoul	Hymn to Tourach	City of Brass
Ashen Ghoul	Hymn to Tourach	City of Brass
Ashen Ghoul	Hymn to Tourach	Mountain
Pocket 3	Pocket 3	Pocket 3
Nether Shadow	Lightning Bolt	Mountain
Nether Shadow	Lightning Bolt	Swamp
Nether Shadow	Lightning Bolt	Swamp
Nether Shadow	Lightning Bolt	Swamp
Pocket 4	Pocket 4	Pocket 4
Knight of Stromgald	Incinerate	Swamp
Knight of Stromgald	Incinerate	Swamp
Knight of Stromgald	Fireball	Swamp
Knight of Stromgald	Fireball	Swamp
Pocket 5	Pocket 5	Pocket 5
Mindstab Thrull	Dark Ritual	Swamp
Mindstab Thrull	Dark Ritual	Swamp
Mindstab Thrull	Dark Ritual	Swamp
Order of the Ebon Hand	Dark Ritual	Swamp

1. Gloom
2. Gloom
3. Gloom
4. Gloom
5. Stench of Evil
6. Stench of Evil
7. Stench of Evil
8. Pryoblast
9. Pryoblast
10. Energy Flux
11. Energy Flux
12. Energy Flux
13. Nevinyrral's Disk
14. Nevinyrral's Disk
15. Nevinyrral's Disk

Use Glooms against White decks, Pyroblasts for Control Magics, and Energy Fluxes for Artifact intensive decks.

The Weird Hippy Shakes is a deck that I put together to take advantage of the Ashen Ghouls and Nether Shadow's special ability to enter play from the graveyard. If a Weirding enters into play, an opponent can deny you your Ghouls and Nether Shadows, but they will return as the game progresses. What fun to play with the undead! The other creatures are present to pressure an opponent early in the game while gearing up for a Weirding.

This deck has a few weaknesses. The first of these is that it suffers to Swords to Plowshares. If an opponent targets the Ghouls with his Swords to Plowshares, it is sometimes best to Bolt them to keep them in the graveyard. While this is an extreme measure, in the late game you can recover from your loss in card count economy because the Ghoul can return to play.

Deck Name: The Weird Bottle Deck

Block One	Block Two	Block Three
Pocket 1	Pocket 1	Pocket 1
Lightning Bolt	Elkin Bottle	City of Brass
Lightning Bolt	Elkin Bottle	City of Brass
Lightning Bolt	Elkin Bottle	City of Brass
Lightning Bolt	Elkin Bottle	Karplusan Forest
Pocket 2	Pocket 2	Pocket 2
Incinerate	Zur's Weirding	Karplusan Forest
Incinerate	Zur's Weirding	Karplusan Forest
Incinerate	Sylvan Library	Karplusan Forest
Incinerate	Sylvan Library	Forest

Pocket 3	Pocket 3	Pocket 3
Elvish Archer	Whirling Dervish	Forest
Elvish Archer	Whirling Dervish	Forest
Elvish Archer	Whirling Dervish	Forest
Elvish Archer	Whirling Dervish	Forest
Pocket 4	Pocket 4	Pocket 4
Lhurgoyf	Fireball	Forest
Lhurgoyf	Fireball	Mountain
Lhurgoyf	Fireball	Mountain
Lhurgoyf	Giant Growth	Mountain
Pocket 5	Pocket 5	Pocket 5
Llanowar Elves	Giant Growth	Mountain
Llanowar Elves	Barbed Sextant	Mountain
Llanowar Elves	Barbed Sextant	Mountain
Llanowar Elves	Barbed Sextant	Mountain

Sideboard:

1. Lifeforce	6. Disintegrate	11. Shatter
2. Lifeforce	7. Howling Mine	12. Barbed Sextant
3. Lifeforce	8. Howling Mine	13. Disenchant
4. Lifeforce	9. Howling Mine	14. Disenchant
5. Disintegrate	10. Howling Mine	15. Disenchant

Use Lifeforces and Howling Mines for Hand Destruction decks, Disintegrates for Creature heavy decks, Shatter for Artifact heavy decks, and Disenchant to counter Death Grip.

I constructed this deck to take advantage of the Elkin Bottle when a Weirding is in play. When you activate the Elkin Bottle, it does not actually force you to draw the card you place on it. Because the card is not actually drawn, the Weirding does not affect it. This makes the Bottle quite an effective tool when you play under a Weirding.

The Bottle also works well with the Sylvan Library. If you have a Bottle and a Library out, you can arrange which card you want to draw at the top of the card library. This can also provide a surprise factor if you have no cards in your hand or if the Weirding is in play. For instance, let's say you have a Weirding in play. Your opponent can see that you hold nothing but land in your hand. You have an Elvish Archer in play, and you draw yet another land with your

Sylvan Library. In the card stack of the Library a Giant Growth rests. You place the Giant Growth on top of the deck, then use your Elvish Archer to attack. Your opponent blocks the Archer with the Angel. You then activate the Bottle, draw your Giant Growth, and cast it on the Archer who promptly shoots down one Angel.

This deck can move quickly and be amusing to play. You can usually keep the playing area swept of creatures with your direct damage. This allows you to storm for blitzkrieg damage early with your Archers, Elves, and Dervishes. After awhile, both your creatures and your opponent's creatures stack up in the graveyard. This presents an opportune time for the Lhurgoyf, a creature with power and toughness equal to the number of creatures residing in the graveyard, to enter play to bash your opponent.

Deck Name: Pantages's Homarid Deck

Block One	Block Two	Block Three
Pocket 1	Pocket 1	Pocket 1
Homarid Warrior	Disenchant	Fellwar Stone
Homarid Warrior	Disenchant	City of Brass
Homarid Warrior	Disenchant	City of Brass
Counterspell	Disenchant	City of Brass
Pocket 2	Pocket 2	Pocket 2
Savannah Lions	Jayemdae Tome	Adarkar Wastes
Savannah Lions	Jayemdae Tome	Adarkar Wastes
Savannah Lions	Jayemdae Tome	Adarkar Wastes
Savannah Lions	Recall	Adarkar Wastes
Pocket 3	Pocket 3	Pocket 3
Mishra's Factory	Swords to Plowshares	Strip Mine
Mishra's Factory	Swords to Plowshares	Strip Mine
Mishra's Factory	Swords to Plowshares	Plains
Mishra's Factory	Swords to Plowshares	Plains
Pocket 4	Pocket 4	Pocket 4
Lightning Bolt	Counterspell	Plains
Lightning Bolt	Counterspell	Island
Lightning Bolt	Disrupting Scepter	Island

Lightning Bolt	Disrupting Scepter	Island
Pocket 5	Pocket 5	Pocket 5
Fireball	Zuran Orb	Island
Fireball	Fellwar Stone	Mountain
Zur's Weirding	Fellwar Stone	Mountain
Zur's Weirding	Fellwar Stone	Mountain

Sideboard:

1. Binding Grasp	6. C.O.P. Red	11. Divine Offering
2. Binding Grasp	7. C.O.P. Red	12. Divine Offering
3. Binding Grasp	8. C.O.P. Red	13. Disenchant
4. Deflection	9. Jester's Cap	14. Fireball
5. Deflection	10. Divine Offering	15. Fireball

Chris constructed this deck after I showed him a very early version of the Engine. He eventually left it for his, the more reliable White/Red deck both he and Wiseman play (see Chapter 9). The Homarid Warriors are a delightful twist, creatures not commonly seen. Their immunity to any spell that targets them for the turn makes them an asset in a Weirding deck.

Regardless of the effectiveness of a Weirding deck in Type II, they are one of the more enjoyable deck types. The Weirding subgame is a nice change from the standard hack, slash, and counter monotony of many duels.

The Weirding is one of the few cards in the Type II pool that will provide a lock. If at any point you are able to net-two-life a round and your opponent draws only one card per round, you can deny him every card he draws.

Chapter 12:

Winter Orb Decks

One of Magic's most recognized game-altering cards is the Winter Orb. The Winter Orb changes the pace of the game. In some situations the Winter Orb can lock down the game and ensure victory for its controller.

Winter Orb decks have diminished in might since the restriction of the Black Vise. Without a Black Vise in play, no quick victories arise for the Winter Orb player. Yet even with a restricted Vise, the Winter Orb is among the most powerful artifacts in the game.

Deck Name: The Orb Sleight/Knight Deck

Block One	Block Two	Block Three
Pocket 1	Pocket 1	Pocket 1
Icy Manipulator	Savannah Lions	Adarkar Wastes
Icy Manipulator	Savannah Lions	Adarkar Wastes
Icy Manipulator	Savannah Lions	Adarkar Wastes
Icy Manipulator	Savannah Lions	Adarkar Wastes
Pocket 2	Pocket 2	Pocket 2
Winter Orb	Swords to Plowshares	Land Cap
Winter Orb	Swords to Plowshares	City of Brass
Winter Orb	Swords to Plowshares	Plains
Kismet	Swords to Plowshares	Plains

Pocket 3	Pocket 3	Pocket 3
Order of Leitbur	Disenchant	Plains
Order of Leitbur	Disenchant	Plains
Order of Leitbur	Disenchant	Plains
Order of Leitbur	Balance	Plains
Pocket 4	Pocket 4	Pocket 4
Order of the White Shield	Power Sink	Plains
Order of the White Shield	Power Sink	Plains
Order of the White Shield	Recall	Plains
Order of the White Shield	Zuran Orb	Plains
Pocket 5	Pocket 5	Pocket 5
White Knight	Fellwar Stone	Plains
Sleight of Mind	Fellwar Stone	Plains
Sleight of Mind	Fellwar Stone	Plains
Sleight of Mind	Fellwar Stone	Plains

Sideboard:

1. Disenchant
2. Divine Offering
3. Divine Offering
4. Divine Offering
5. Armageddon
6. Karma
7. Karma
8. C.O.P. Red
9. C.O.P. Red
10. C.O.P. Red
11. C.O.P. White
12. C.O.P. White
13. C.O.P. White
14. White Knight
15. Black Vise

Use Disenchant for Artifact decks, Armageddon for Mana-dependent decks and Tome decks, Karma for Black decks, C.O.P. Reds for Red Decks, C.O.P. Whites for White decks, and White Knight for Tweak decks.

The Sleight/Knight theme works well in the Winter Orb environment. All of the spells accompanying the Sleight/Knight theme cost little, and therefore, cast cheaply when under the Winter Orb. The optimal situation to release a Winter Orb into the game is by forcing your opponent to tap out while an Icy Manipulator and Kismet are in play. Then, on your turn, you lock up the land they untap during their upkeep with the Icy. From that point on, unless they have Crumble in their deck which costs only one green mana, they have no hope for success.

There are a few small tricks that you will want to familiarize yourself with while using the Knight/Sleight deck. You should not use your Sleights on the Knights until your opponent targets them.

Your aim is to force him to waste his spell on trying to eliminate the Knight. This deck operates on attrition theory. If you play a Knight, you should not have more than one in play at a time. This deck can suffer poor card economy against cards like Pyroclasym, but only if you allow your opponent to grab that advantage.

Deck Name: Ernham Orb Deck

Block One	Block Two	Block Three
Pocket 1	Pocket 1	Pocket 1
Icy Manipulator	Ernham Djinn	Fellwar Stone
Icy Manipulator	Ernham Djinn	Fellwar Stone
Icy Manipulator	Ernham Djinn	City of Brass
Disenchant	Ernham Djinn	City of Brass
Pocket 2	Pocket 2	Pocket 2
Winter Orb	Elvish Archer	City of Brass
Winter Orb	Elvish Archer	Brushland
Winter Orb	Elvish Archer	Brushland
Kismet	Elvish Archer	Brushland
Pocket 3	Pocket 3	Pocket 3
Swords to Plowshares	Savannah Lions	Brushland
Swords to Plowshares	Savannah Lions	Karplusan Forest
Swords to Plowshares	Savannah Lions	Mountain
Fireball	Savannah Lions	Mountain
Pocket 4	Pocket 4	Pocket 4
Incinerate	Serra Angel	Mountain
Incinerate	Serra Angel	Mountain
Disenchant	Mishra's Factory	Mountain
Fireball	Mishra's Factory	Plains
Pocket 5	Pocket 5	Pocket 5
Lightning Bolt	Mishra's Factory	Plains
Lightning Bolt	Mishra's Factory	Plains
Lightning Bolt	Fellwar Stone	Plains
Lightning Bolt	Fellwar Stone	Plains

Sideboard:

1. Disenchant	6. Icy Manipulator	11. Fireball
2. Disenchant	7. Tranquility	12. Pyroblast
3. Divine Offering	8. Tranquility	13. Pyroblast
4. Divine Offering	9. Tranquility	14. Pyroblast
5. Divine Offering	10. Fireball	15. Pyroblast

Use Disenchant for Artifact intensive decks, Icy Manipulator and Fireballs for Tweak decks, Tranquilities for Gloom decks, and Pyroblasts for Blue decks.

I originally constructed this deck to mock the early Kird Ape deck which contained fourteen Kird Apes and fourteen Lightning Bolts. Experimentation revealed the deck floundered in the mid and late game. The Winter Orb theme then integrated into the deck. The Winter Orb served two purposes. In the early game, it slowed opponents down to a point where they could not react fast enough to all of the Ernham Orb deck's early game creatures. In the late game, it provided an opportunity to lock down an opponent.

Deck Name: Winter Fire in the Swamp

Block One	Block Two	Block Three
Pocket 1	Pocket 1	Pocket 1
Winter Orb	Orgg	Fellwar Stone
Winter Orb	Orgg	City of Brass
Winter Orb	Orgg	City of Brass
Black Vise	Disenchant	Sulfurous Springs
Pocket 2	Pocket 2	Pocket 2
Icy Manipulator	Foul Familiar	Sulfurous Springs
Icy Manipulator	Foul Familiar	Sulfurous Springs
Icy Manipulator	Foul Familiar	Sulfurous Springs
Icy Manipulator	Foul Familiar	Swamp
Pocket 3	Pocket 3	Pocket 3
Paralyze	Knights of Stromgald	Swamp
Paralyze	Knights of Stromgald	Swamp
Paralyze	Dark Ritual	Swamp
Paralyze	Dark Ritual	Swamp

Pocket 4	Pocket 4	Pocket 4
Lightning Bolt	Disenchant	Swamp
Lightning Bolt	Dark Ritual	Swamp
Lightning Bolt	Barbed Sextant	Swamp
Lightning Bolt	Barbed Sextant	Swamp
Pocket 5	Pocket 5	Pocket 5
Incinerate	Barbed Sextant	Mountain
Incinerate	Barbed Sextant	Mountain
Incinerate	Fellwar Stone	Mountain
Incinerate	Fellwar Stone	Mountain

Sideboard:

1. Gloom	6. Pyroblast	11. Hymn to Tourach
2. Gloom	7. Shatter	12. Hymn to Tourach
3. Gloom	8. Shatter	13. Disrupting Scepter
4. Gloom	9. Hymn to Tourach	14. Rack
5. Pryoblast	10. Hymn to Tourach	15. Rack

Use Glooms against White decks, Pyroblasts against Blue decks, Shatters against Artifact reliant decks, and Hymn to Touraches against Transformational decks.

This deck ranks as one of the more entertaining Tier One decks. There is a great deal of symmetry within this deck's architecture. The Paralyze effectively eliminates a creature when a Winter Orb rests in play. If you have a Paralyze and an Icy Manipulator in play, you can torment an opponent by tapping his creature immediately after he pays four mana during his upkeep to untap it.

The direct damage and the Paralyze are simply for creature control. They clear the board while the Foul Familiars, Knights, and Orggs commit their detestable acts. The sideboard overflows with hand destruction to change the strategy of the game on an opponent. This operates nicely if during the first game you find you cannot overtake him.

The secret to this deck is to keep an opponent's creatures locked down or in the graveyard. Your Orggs and Foul Familiars will pound out an early victory if your opponent cannot deal with them in a timely manner. Beware though, Serra Angels punish this deck for its wickedness.

Deck Name: Critter Orb Deck

Block One	Block Two	Block Three
Pocket 1	Pocket 1	Pocket 1
Llanowar Elves	Autumn Willow	Karplusan Forest
Llanowar Elves	Autumn Willow	Karplusan Forest
Llanowar Elves	Fireball	Karplusan Forest
Llanowar Elves	Fireball	Karplusan Forest
Pocket 2	Pocket 2	Pocket 2
Fyndhorn Elves	Icy Manipulator	Forest
Fyndhorn Elves	Icy Manipulator	Forest
Fyndhorn Elves	Icy Manipulator	Forest
Fyndhorn Elves	Icy Manipulator	Forest
Pocket 3	Pocket 3	Pocket 3
Elvish Archers	Winter Orb	Mountain
Elvish Archers	Winter Orb	Mountain
Elvish Archers	Winter Orb	Mountain
Elvish Archers	Sylvan Library	Forest
Pocket 4	Pocket 4	Pocket 4
Lhurgoyf	Mishra's Factory	Forest
Lhurgoyf	Mishra's Factory	Forest
Lhurgoyf	Mishra's Factory	Forest
Fireball	Mishra's Factory	Forest
Pocket 5	Pocket 5	Pocket 5
Ernham Djinn	Fellwar Stone	Forest
Ernham Djinn	Fellwar Stone	Forest
Ernham Djinn	Fellwar Stone	Forest
Ernham Djinn	Fellwar Stone	Forest

Sideboard:

1. Pyroblast
2. Pyroblast
3. Pyroblast
4. Pyroblast
5. Red Elemental Blast
6. Red Elemental Blast
7. Lifeforce
8. Lifeforce
9. Lifeforce
10. Tranquility
11. Tranquility
12. Tranquility
13. Crumble
14. Crumble
15. Crumble

Use Pyroblasts against Control Magics, Lifeforces against Black decks, and Crumbles against Artifact heavy decks.

The Critter Orb deck utilizes the mana producing Elves to sustain itself while under the influence of the Orb. Though cards like Earthquake and Pyroclasym harm this deck, it stores so many creatures that once several enter the graveyard, the trudge of a Lhurgoyf's feet becomes deafening. It is not uncommon for these beasts to attain the double digits in power and toughness.

Chapter 13:

Stasis Decks

Stasis is one of the few cards in the game that can generate a lock, that is a situation your opponent cannot possibly win, on a match. Because of its power to disembowel an opponent's deck, all tournament level players should familiarize themselves with how it functions and recognize its strengths and weaknesses.

Cards That Work Well in Stasis Decks

White
1. Arenson's Aura
2. Disenchant
3. Kismet
4. Land Tax
5. Serra Angel
6. Trade Caravan

Blue
1. Boomerang
2. Hurkyl's Recall
3. Mana Short
4. Power Sink
5. Stasis
6. Time Elemental
7. Zephyr Falcon

Green
1. Birds of Paradise
2. Instill Energy
3. Juniper Order
   Druid
4. Ley Druid

Red
1. Disintegrate
2. Fireball
3. Lava Burst
4. Pyroblast
5. Red Elemental Blast

Black
1. Ghost Hounds

Artifacts
1. Black Vise
2. Yotian Soldier
3. Zuran Orb

Stasis is a powerful card because it allots its controller time. It has the potential to force both players out of the early game and into the mid game. This can benefit the Stasis player if he plays against a resource denial deck (Land Destruction or Hand Destruction) that attempts to seize victories in the early game. Stasis prevents this, carrying the match into the mid game, where it can often achieve a lock on the match.

Stasis prohibits the untap phase. Reaping rewards from this card depends upon two strategies. You must either find methods to escape the card's effect for yourself, while ensuring that your opponent does not escape; or you must utilize cards that do not suffer from the absence of the untap phase.

Many methods exist to achieve a Stasis lock, but unfortunately, they are all very fragile. A sturdy partial lock is to use Stasis in conjunction with Zuran Orb and Land Tax, both of which are durable and independently valuable. You can cast a Zuran Orb and a Land Tax, and then sacrifice enough land so you have less than your opponent. Then, you can search through your library for Islands. Now you can cast a Stasis and maintain it until you remove all of the Islands from your deck, thus effectively eliminating the upkeep phase. This situation creates difficulties for an opponent if he is suffering to a Black Vise. Recall, however, that the Zuran Orb's restriction severely diluted this combination's potency.

There are a number of other ways to try and create the Stasis lock. Most of them involve the use of creatures which opponents easily remove. Consequently, a competitive Stasis style deck remains a difficult work to construct.

Deck Name: The Time Trap

Block One	Block Two	Block Three
Pocket 1	Pocket 1	Pocket 1
Power Sink	Disenchant	Adarkar Wastes
Power Sink	Disenchant	Adarkar Wastes
Power Sink	Disenchant	Adarkar Wastes
Power Sink	Disenchant	Adarkar Wastes
Pocket 2	Pocket 2	Pocket 2

Stasis	Serra Angel	City of Brass
Stasis	Serra Angel	Island
Stasis	Serra Angel	Island
Stasis	Kismet	Island
Pocket 3	Pocket 3	Pocket 3
Black Vise	Swords to Plowshares	Island
Yotian Soldier	Swords to Plowshares	Island
Yotian Soldier	Swords to Plowshares	Island
Yotian Soldier	Swords to Plowshares	Island
Pocket 4	Pocket 4	Pocket 4
Time Elemental	Zuran Orb	Island
Time Elemental	Despotic Scepter	Island
Recall	Land Tax	Island
Balance	Land Tax	Plains
Pocket 5	Pocket 5	Pocket 5
Howling Mine	Land Tax	Plains
Howling Mine	Wrath of God	Plains
Howling Mine	Wrath of God	Plains
Ivory Tower	Counterspell	Plains

Sideboard:

1. Counterspell
2. Counterspell
3. Howling Mine
4. Karma
5. Karma
6. Karma
7. Divine Offering
8. Divine Offering
9. Island Sanctuary
10. Island Sanctuary
11. Island Sanctuary
12. Circle of Protection Red
13. Circle of Protection Red
14. Circle of Protection Red
15. Circle of Protection Red

Use the Counterspells for general use, Howling Mine for Hand Destruction decks, Divine Offerings for Heavy Artifact decks, Island Sanctuaries for Weenie Creature decks, and Circle of Protection Reds for Red damage decks.

This is a fairly simple Stasis deck with impressive reactive ability and like most Stasis decks possesses many defenses against various deck types. The Howling Mines provide fortification against Hand Destruction decks. The Power Sinks counter any type of Large Fast Creature deck or Burn deck. The Land Taxes are a great help against Land Destruction decks. The Stasis deck can suffer against Weenie decks. In many cases, a Weenie deck will steamroll the Stasis deck before it can ever assume a position of control.

The purpose of the Time Elemental in this deck is to generate an infinite Stasis lock. All you need do is cast Kismet early, followed by a Time Elemental. When both of these are in play, you wait until you hold both a Stasis and a Power Sink in hand and six mana on the table. Then when your opponent casts something, you Power Sink him. Once he taps out, you play your Stasis. Any new land he puts into play will enter play tapped. During his end phase you pay two blue and two other to activate your Time Elemental and pick up the Stasis. Though it is unlikely that you will achieve this position, if you accomplish it, your opponent faces certain defeat with no chance of recovery.

Deck Name: The SFD (Stasis Fireball Deck)

Block One	Block Two	Block Three
Pocket 1	Pocket 1	Pocket 1
Stasis	Lightning Bolt	Mountain
Stasis	Lightning Bolt	Mountain
Stasis	Lightning Bolt	Mountain
Stasis	Lightning Bolt	Mountain
Pocket 2	Pocket 2	Pocket 2
Fireball	Incinerate	Mountain
Fireball	Incinerate	Mountain
Fireball	Incinerate	Island
Fireball	Incinerate	Island
Pocket 3	Pocket 3	Pocket 3
Howling Mine	Disenchant	Adarkar Wastes
Howling Mine	Disenchant	Adarkar Wastes
Howling Mine	Disenchant	Adarkar Wastes
Howling Mine	Zuran Orb	Adarkar Wastes
Pocket 4	Pocket 4	Pocket 4
Power Sink	Nevinyrral's Disk	Island
Power Sink	Nevinyrral's Disk	Island
Power Sink	Counterspell	Island
Power Sink	Counterspell	Island
Pocket 5	Pocket 5	Pocket 5

Black Vise	City of Brass	Island
Ivory Tower	City of Brass	Island
Serra Angel	City of Brass	Island
Serra Angel	Mountain	Island

Sideboard:

1. Hydroblast
2. Hydroblast
3. Hydroblast
4. Pyroblast
5. Pyroblast
6. Pyroblast
7. Pyroclasym
8. Pyroclasym
9. Pyroclasym
10. Shatter
11. Shatter
12. Shatter
13. Control Magic
14. Control Magic
15. Control Magic

Use the Hydroblasts against Red decks, Pyroblasts against Blue decks, Pyroclasms for Small Creature decks, Shatters for Artifact decks, and Control Magics for Large Creature decks.

The SFD is a Burn/Stasis/Counterspell deck. In the early game you use your direct damage to eliminate your opponent's creatures until you draw a Stasis. If you have a Stasis in hand and enough mana to fuel it, you allow your opponent to take his next turn. If you have a Power Sink in hand, you counter whatever he casts and force him to tap out. When your turn comes, you play a Stasis. For several turns you continue to pay for Stasis as long as you can. Then, after you exhaust almost all of your blue sources of mana, cast a Disenchant on your own Stasis during your opponent's end phase. By this time you should have built up a large amount of mana sources. Now, if luck permits, you can finish your opponent with a large Fireball.

Deck Name: The Trade Caravan Deck

Block One	Block Two	Block Three
Pocket 1	Pocket 1	Pocket 1
Trade Caravan	Zephyr Falcon	Adarkar Wastes
Trade Caravan	Zephyr Falcon	Adarkar Wastes
Trade Caravan	Zephyr Falcon	Adarkar Wastes
Trade Caravan	Zephyr Falcon	Adarkar Wastes
Pocket 2	Pocket 2	Pocket 2
Stasis	Serra Angel	Island
Stasis	Serra Angel	Island

Stasis	Disenchant	Island
Stasis	Disenchant	Island
Pocket 3	Pocket 3	Pocket 3
Savannah Lions	Disenchant	Island
Savannah Lions	Disenchant	Island
Savannah Lions	Swords to Plowshares	Island
Savannah Lions	Swords to Plowshares	Island
Pocket 4	Pocket 4	Pocket 4
Yotian Soldier	Swords to Plowshares	Island
Yotian Soldier	Swords to Plowshares	Island
Yotian Soldier	Unstable Mutation	Plains
Black Vise	Unstable Mutation	Plains
Pocket 5	Pocket 5	Pocket 5
Howling Mine	Power Sink	Plains
Howling Mine	Power Sink	Plains
Howling Mine	City of Brass	Plains
Power Sink	City of Brass	Plains

Sideboard:

1. C.O.P. Red	6. Land Tax	11. Divine Offering
2. C.O.P. Red	7. Island Sanctuary	12. Disenchant
3. C.O.P. Red	8. Island Sanctuary	13. Disenchant
4. Land Tax	9. Island Sanctuary	14. Control Magic
5. Land Tax	10. Howling Mine	15. Control Magic

Use C.O.P. Reds against Burn decks, Land Taxes for Land Destruction decks, Island Sanctuaries for Small Creature decks, Howling Mine for Hand Destruction decks, Divine Offering for Artifact intensive decks, and Control Magics for Large Creature decks and those with Serra Angels.

This deck uses the Trade Caravans to generate a continuous Stasis. The Trade Caravans allow their controller to exchange trade tokens that he accumulates to untap lands during the opponent's upkeep. If there are two Caravans in play you can maintain a permanent Stasis and the game will continue with no untap phase. Realistically, though, an opponent is likely to have some form of creature removal and it is unlikely that you will keep the Caravan in play. But this deck has enough creatures that an opponent may falter or experience difficulty in determining the threats of the deck.

Chapter 14:

Changes in the Five Basic Decks

The strength of the various decks that fall under the category of the five basic decks differs from Type I to Type II. In Type I, Land Destruction and Counterspell decks dominate the five basic decks. In Type II however, the dominant basic deck forms are Hand Destruction, Burn, and Fast Creature decks.

Most versions of the five basic decks are Tier Two decks. If one of the FBDs (Five Basic Decks) manages to attain the First Tier, it is usually a Hand Destruction or a Fast Creature deck. Players can cut some of these decks to make them of Tier One power, but most of them will fail to achieve the semifinals in a Swiss-style tournament.

Nonetheless, these are the most common deck types in most tournaments. They are easy to construct and easier to play. Many inexperienced players play decks like these and play them well. It is not uncommon for a Tier One quality deck to fall to pieces in a tournament because of a defect against one of the five basic decks.

As a strong and experienced tournament player, you should not only design your deck with the FBDs in mind, but you should construct these decks and play against them. I frequently scrap deck ideas because of obvious defects against one of the five basic decks. In most cases, you will find that your deck performs extremely well against a few of these decks, and mediocre against others. The goal to strive for is about a sixty percent success rate against each of these decks. This means that when you sit down at the tournament across from someone playing one of these decks (and you will face these decks) you will have a greater chance for victory than your opponent.

Land Destruction

Cards That Work Well in Type II Land Destruction Decks

Artifacts	Land	Blue
1. Ankh of Mishra	1. Strip Mine	1. Energy Flux
2. Black Vise	2. Power Sink	
3. Dingus Egg	3. Zur's Weirding	**White**
4. Icy Manipulator		1. Armageddon
5. Jester's Cap		2. Brainwash
6. Jeweled Amulet		

Black	Red	Green
1. Blight	1. Incinerate	1. Birds of Paradise
2. Dark Ritual	2. Lightning Bolt	2. Fyndhorn Elves
3. Gloom	3. Mudslide	3. Llanowar Elves
4. Icequake	4. Pyrotechnics	4. Stunted Growth
5. Mole Worms	5. Stone Rain	5. Thermokarst
6. Paralyze	6. Wild Growth	
7. Seizures		
8. Stench of Evil		

Land destruction is much slower and less effective in Type II than in Type I. Without the Nether Void in Type II tournaments, Land Destruction decks lose consistently to Small Creature decks because their land destruction spells cannot impede the constant barrage of small creatures. Small Creature decks overrun a Land Destruction deck.

Even if a Land Destruction deck supplements itself with a large amount of direct damage and creature removal, the land destruction element is almost useless because most spells in Small Fast Creature decks do not cost more than two mana each.

Deck Name: FBD Red/Green Land Destruction

Block One	Block Two	Block Three
Pocket 1	Pocket 1	Pocket 1
Ernham Djinn	Stone Rain	Barbed Sextant
Ernham Djinn	Stone Rain	Barbed Sextant
Ernham Djinn	Stone Rain	Barbed Sextant
Ernham Djinn	Stone Rain	Barbed Sextant
Pocket 2	Pocket 2	Pocket 2
Llanowar Elves	Thermokarst	Karplusan Forest
Llanowar Elves	Thermokarst	Karplusan Forest
Llanowar Elves	Thermokarst	Karplusan Forest
Llanowar Elves	Thermokarst	Karplusan Forest
Pocket 3	Pocket 3	Pocket 3
Fyndhorn Elves	Black Vise	City of Brass
Fyndhorn Elves	Ankh of Mishra	Mountain
Shivan Dragon	Ankh of Mishra	Mountain
Shivan Dragon	Autumn Willow	Mountain
Pocket 4	Pocket 4	Pocket 4
Detonate	Lightning Bolt	Mountain
Detonate	Lightning Bolt	Forest
Detonate	Lightning Bolt	Forest
Sylvan Library	Lightning Bolt	Forest
Pocket 5	Pocket 5	Pocket 5
Fireball	Mishra's Factory	Forest
Fireball	Mishra's Factory	Forest
Fireball	Mishra's Factory	Forest
Fireball	Mishra's Factory	Forest

Sideboard:

1. Shatter
2. Shatter
3. Tranquility
4. Tranquility
5. Incinerate
6. Incinerate
7. Incinerate
8. Flashfires
9. Flashfires
10. Flashfires
11. Flashfires
12. Whirling Dervish
13. Whirling Dervish
14. Whirling Dervish
15. Whirling Dervish

Use the Shatters for Artifact decks, Tranquilities for C.O.P. Red decks, Incinerates for Hypnotic Specter/Mindstab/Order of Leitbur, Flashfires for White decks, and Whirling Dervishes for Black decks.

This deck is a basic Red/Green Land Destruction deck with Elves to provide an opportunity for second turn land destruction. Although it is unlikely that this deck has much of a chance against a White Weenie deck in the first game of the match, it generates much better odds in the second game. In the second game, the controller of this deck can sideboard in the Flashfires and Incinerates. When you follow this path of action, you typically hold your single shot land destruction, that is land destruction that trades one card for one card, until you draw a Flashfires. You must rebuff their creature hoard with your direct damage. Remember though, after you cast the Flashfires you should hold enough land destruction in hand to kill each land an opponent drops into play.

There are a number of ways to play this deck. The way you play it depends on your draw. If you draw a number of land destruction spells and a Black Vise, then your goal may be to concentrate on all of an opponent's early land, trying to kill him with an early supported Vise. The second option is one you might take when you only draw one or two land destruction spells. Then, you simply concentrate on what you believe to be the most threatening mana producers in your opponent's deck. With twelve land destruction, you can usually weaken a deck's primary color, or almost eliminate their secondary color.

There is an Achilles' heel to Red/Green Land Destruction decks: they commonly rely on Elves for fast mana and second-turn land destruction. If you can manage to remove the Elves, you give yourself another turn to develop before the land destruction starts. This is extremely important if you use Fellwar Stones, which are useful against Land Destruction decks. Land Destruction decks infrequently contain many artifact destruction spells. For example, if your opponent goes first and manages to cast an Elf, he can remove your first land before you can play your second land to cast a Fellwar Stone. If you Bolt the opponent's Elf you can cast the Fellwar Stone and thus have a more reliable source of mana.

Regardless of how you approach it, you need to prepare for Land Destruction decks. While Land Destruction decks are not as common as some of the other five basic decks, they will pop up in tournaments and knock out those players who fail to prepare for them.

Deck Name: The Black/Red FBD Land Destruction Deck

Block One	Block Two	Block Three
Pocket 1	Pocket 1	Pocket 1
Icequake	Order of the Ebon Hand	Sulfurous Springs
Icequake	Order of the Ebon Hand	Sulfurous Springs
Icequake	Icy Manipulator	Sulfurous Springs
Icequake	Icy Manipulator	Sulfurous Springs
Pocket 2	Pocket 2	Pocket 2
Stone Rain	Knights of Stromgald	Mountain
Stone Rain	Knights of Stromgald	Mountain
Stone Rain	Knights of Stromgald	Mountain
Stone Rain	Knights of Stromgald	Mountain
Pocket 3	Pocket 3	Pocket 3
Strip Mine	Vampire	Mountain
Strip Mine	Vampire	Mountain
Strip Mine	Vampire	Swamp
Strip Mine	Vampire	Swamp
Pocket 4	Pocket 4	Pocket 4
Lightning Bolt	Black Vise	Swamp
Lightning Bolt	Incinerate	Swamp
Lightning Bolt	Incinerate	Swamp
Lightning Bolt	Incinerate	Swamp
Pocket 5	Pocket 5	Pocket 5
Pyrotechnics	Jeweled Amulet	Swamp
Pyrotechnics	Jeweled Amulet	Swamp
Paralyze	Jeweled Amulet	Swamp
Paralyze	Jeweled Amulet	Swamp

Sideboard:

1. Shatter
2. Shatter
3. Shatter
4. Detonate
5. Detonate
6. Detonate
7. Paralyze
8. Paralyze
9. Pyrotechnics
10. Pyrotechnics
11. Gloom
12. Gloom
13. Gloom
14. Flashfires
15. Flashfires

The Red/Black Land Destruction deck is actually much closer to Tier One status than its counterpart, the Red/Green. The Red/Black Land Destruction deck is more adept at dealing with swarms of small, banding white creatures. With six Knights, the only real threat to the Black/Red are the White Knights, which opponents can easily eliminate with the deck's four Lightning Bolts and two Pyrotechnics. This deck also contains fewer flaws than the Red/Green. One reason this deck is more reliable than the Red/Green is its more dependable sources of fast mana. It is much more likely that an opponent will use a Lightning Bolt on a Llanowar Elves than waste one of his three or four Disenchants on a Jeweled Amulet.

The Red/Black deck reserves better resources for dealing with the more threatening colors to a Land Destruction deck than the Red/Green deck. Black provides many good counters to white, which can present problems for a Land Destruction deck. The Knights stand as the main difference in quality between the two decks.

Counterspell Decks

Cards That Work Well in a Counterspell Deck

Artifacts	Land	Blue
1. Barbed Sextant	1. Mishra's Factory	1. Counterspell
2. Fountain of Youth		2. Deflection
3. Icy Manipulator		3. Memory Lapse
4. Ivory Tower		4. Portent
6. Urza's Bauble		5. Power Sink
		6. Recall
White		7. Spell Blast
1. Disenchant		8. Zur's Weirding
2. Divine Offering		
3. Swords to Plowshares		

Counterspell decks are quickly regaining the status in Type II that they enjoyed in Type I. Many of these decks are very slow and very vulnerable to an early Vise. But with the Duelists' Convocation restriction of the Black Vise, these decks present a much deadlier threat than they once did. The Decks still display problems with Small White Creature decks. In Type I, Counterspell decks have the advantage of faster mana, not to mention the all powerful Mana Drain, the Abyss, and the Moat. In Type II, such resources do not exist.

Deck Name: FBD Blue/White Counterspell

Block One	Block Two	Block Three
Pocket 1	Pocket 1	Pocket 1
Counterspell	Control Magic	Adarkar Wastes
Counterspell	Control Magic	Adarkar Wastes
Counterspell	Control Magic	Adarkar Wastes
Counterspell	Control Magic	Adarkar Wastes
Pocket 2	Pocket 2	Pocket 2
Power Sink	Balance	City of Brass
Power Sink	Serra Angel	City of Brass
Power Sink	Serra Angel	City of Brass
Power Sink	Recall	Plains
Pocket 3	Pocket 3	Pocket 3
Spell Blast	Ghost Ship	Plains
Spell Blast	Ghost Ship	Plains
Spell Blast	Ghost Ship	Plains
Ivory Tower	Zuran Orb	Island
Pocket 4	Pocket 4	Pocket 4
Disenchant	Mishra's Factory	Island
Disenchant	Mishra's Factory	Island
Disenchant	Mishra's Factory	Island
Disenchant	Mishra's Factory	Island
Pocket 5	Pocket 5	Pocket 5
Swords to Plowshares	Barbed Sextant	Island
Swords to Plowshares	Barbed Sextant	Island
Swords to Plowshares	Barbed Sextant	Island
Swords to Plowshares	Barbed Sextant	Island

Sideboard:

1. Hydroblast	6. Divine Offering	11. Wrath of God
2. Hydroblast	7. Divine Offering	12. C.O.P. White
3. Deflection	8. Divine Offering	13. C.O.P. White
4. Deflection	9. Wrath of God	14. C.O.P. White
5. Divine Offering	10. Wrath of God	15. C.O.P. Black

Use the Hydroblasts against Red decks, Divine Offerings for Artifact intensive decks, Wrath of Gods for Small Creature decks, C.O.P. Whites for White Small Creature decks, and C.O.P. Black against Black decks.

The Blue/White Counterspell deck is the most common form for a Counterspell deck. These decks exhibit impressive power, that is if they can live past the first three turns. Early creatures can create nightmares for Counterspell decks, the kind that don't and won't leave a Counterspell deck controller alone. These decks perform best against Burn decks or large creature decks. Many times, Small Creature decks will generate too many creatures for the Blue/White Counterspell deck to handle.

One of the greatest threats to a Counterspell deck is Strip Mines. Counterspell players cannot Counter, Disenchant, Plowshare, or otherwise remove a Strip Mine. These cards will cause any blue mage to shudder. No longer can a blue mage feel secure with only two untapped blue mana available.

A great deficiency in Counterspell decks is that they must always react to an opponent's actions. This means that they must constantly leave mana untapped in order to use a Counterspell, Power Sink, Deflect, or Spell Blast. One of the persistent difficulties with these decks is that they must often gamble, tapping out to cast a creature or permanent while leaving themselves vulnerable and unable to counter for the opponent's turn.

Deck Name: FBD Red/Blue Counterspell

Block One	Block Two	Block Three
Pocket 1	Pocket 1	Pocket 1
Counterspell	Fireball	City of Brass
Counterspell	Fireball	City of Brass

Counterspell	Control Magic	City of Brass
Counterspell	Control Magic	Mountain
Pocket 2	Pocket 2	Pocket 2
Spell Blast	Ghost Ship	Mountain
Spell Blast	Ghost Ship	Mountain
Deflection	Ghost Ship	Mountain
Deflection	Ghost Ship	Mountain
Pocket 3	Pocket 3	Pocket 3
Power Sink	Azure Drake	Island
Power Sink	Azure Drake	Island
Power Sink	Disenchant	Island
Recall	Disenchant	Island
Pocket 4	Pocket 4	Pocket 4
Lightning Bolt	Barbed Sextant	Island
Lightning Bolt	Barbed Sextant	Island
Lightning Bolt	Barbed Sextant	Island
Lightning Bolt	Barbed Sextant	Island
Pocket 5	Pocket 5	Pocket 5
Incinerate	Jeweled Amulet	Island
Incinerate	Jeweled Amulet	Island
Incinerate	Jeweled Amulet	Island
Incinerate	Jeweled Amulet	Island

Sideboard:

1. Pyroclasym	6. Shatter	11. Pyroblast
2. Pyroclasym	7. Shatter	12. Pyroblast
3. Pyroclasym	8. Shatter	13. Pyroblast
4. Pyroclasym	9. Control	14. Deflection
5. Shatter	10. Control Magic	15. Deflection

Use Pyroclasyms for Small Creature decks, Shatters for Heavy Artifact decks, Control Magics for Hand Destruction decks, Pyroblasts against Blue decks, and Deflections against Red decks.

The Red/Blue Counterspell deck is not subject to as many difficulties as the White/Blue. While using non-aligned colors can pose difficulties, the red/blue mixture allows for a greater variety of roads to victory, plus a larger amount of creature removal. This aids in solving a number of the Counterspell deck's dilemmas.

The four Incinerates and four Lightning Bolts will help clear the board of nuisance creatures. The Barbed Sextants are also great aids in overcoming the Black Vise in these types of decks. If you continually face damaging Vises, you might consider using Urza's Baubles.

Burn Decks

Cards That Work Well in Burn Decks

Artifact
1. Black Vise
2. Fellwar Stone
3. Howling Mine

Land
1. Mishra's Factory

Green
1. Sylvan Library
2. Tinder Wall
3. Tranquility

Blue
1. Deflection

Red
1. Disintegrate
2. Earthquake
3. Fireball
4. Incinerate
5. Lava Burst
6. Lightning Bolt
7. Mana Flare
8. Meteor Shower
9. Orcish Lumberjack
10. Pyrotechnics

White
1. Disenchant
2. Eye for an Eye
3. Repentant Blacksmith

Black
1. Drain Life
2. Soul Burn
3. Terror

Burn decks compare only to Fast Creature decks in their simplicity. While any competent sideboard will shut these decks down, they still present a serious enough threat. These decks benefit from the ability to both eliminate an opponent's creatures and reduce his life with the same spell.

Although they compete adequately against certain deck types, Burn decks contain many problems. Few deck types are so easily shut down as the Burn decks. These decks lack diverse roads to victory and frequently suffer for this defect. No greater nemesis exists for a Burn deck than C.O.P. Red.

Deck Name: The FBD Red/Green Burn Deck

Block One	Block Two	Block Three
Pocket 1	Pocket 1	Pocket 1
Lightning Bolt	Mishra's Factory	Karplusan Forest
Lightning Bolt	Mishra's Factory	Karplusan Forest
Lightning Bolt	Mishra's Factory	Dwarven Ruins
Lightning Bolt	Mishra's Factory	Dwarven Ruins
Pocket 2	Pocket 2	Pocket 2
Incinerate	Pyrotechnics	Dwarven Ruins
Incinerate	Zuran Orb	Dwarven Ruins
Incinerate	Tranquility	Mountain
Incinerate	Tranquility	Mountain
Pocket 3	Pocket 3	Pocket 3
Fireball	Shatter	Mountain
Fireball	Shatter	Mountain
Fireball	Shatter	Mountain
Fireball	Shatter	Mountain
Pocket 4	Pocket 4	Pocket 4
Disintegrate	Barbed Sextant	Mountain
Disintegrate	Barbed Sextant	Mountain
Disintegrate	Barbed Sextant	Mountain
Disintegrate	Barbed Sextant	Mountain
Pocket 5	Pocket 5	Pocket 5
Lava Burst	City of Brass	Mountain
Lava Burst	City of Brass	Mountain
Lava Burst	Karplusan Forest	Mountain
Balance	Karplusan Forest	Mountain

Sideboard:

1. Pyroblast
2. Pyroblast
3. Pyroblast
4. Pyroblast
5. Red Elemental Blast
6. Red Elemental Blast
7. Red Elemental Blast
8. Anarchy
9. Anarchy
10. Anarchy
11. Tranquility
12. Crumble
13. Crumble
14. Detonate
15. Detonate

Use Pyroblast against Blue decks, Anarchy against predominantly White decks, and Crumble against Artifact decks.

This Red/Green Burn deck is very simple; you just singe your opponent. If your opponent plays blue, sideboard in the seven anti-blue cards in your sideboard and transform your deck into an anti-blue counter deck. If he plays with white, call in the Anarchy and third Tranquility.

Deck Name: FBD Red/White Burn Deck

Block One	Block Two	Block Three
Pocket 1	Pocket 1	Pocket 1
Disintegrate	Blinking Spirit	City of Brass
Disintegrate	Blinking Spirit	City of Brass
Disintegrate	Blinking Spirit	City of Brass
Disintegrate	Balance	City of Brass
Pocket 2	Pocket 2	Pocket 2
Fireball	Disenchant	Mountain
Fireball	Disenchant	Mountain
Fireball	Disenchant	Mountain
Fireball	Disenchant	Mountain
Pocket 3	Pocket 3	Pocket 3
Lightning Bolt	Savannah Lions	Mountain
Lightning Bolt	Savannah Lions	Mountain
Lightning Bolt	Savannah Lions	Mountain
Lightning Bolt	Savannah Lions	Mountain
Pocket 4	Pocket 4	Pocket 4
Incinerate	Mishra's Factory	Mountain
Incinerate	Mishra's Factory	Mountain
Incinerate	Mishra's Factory	Plains
Incinerate	Mishra's Factory	Plains
Pocket 5	Pocket 5	Pocket 5
Lava Burst	Barbed Sextant	Plains
Serra Angel	Barbed Sextant	Plains
Serra Angel	Barbed Sextant	Plains
Serra Angel	Barbed Sextant	Plains

Sideboard:

1. Divine Offering	6. Tranquility	11. Pyroblast
2. Divine Offering	7. Tranquility	12. Red Elemental Blast
3. Divine Offering	8. Pyroblast	13. Red Elemental Blast
4. Jester's Cap	9. Pyroblast	14. Deflection
5. Jester's Cap	10. Pyroblast	15. Deflection

Use the Divine Offerings against Artifact intensive decks, Jester's Cap for C.O.P. Red and Gloom, Pyroblasts for Blue decks, and Deflection against Burn decks.

This Red/White Burn deck possesses more depth than the Green/White version. The Red/White enjoys diversified sources of damage which make the C.O.P. Red less threatening. You can use your Burn early as reaction to an opponent's creatures. By invoking this path, you can clear a path for your creatures to attack unblocked. In the late game, one needs to weigh the value of removing an opponent's creatures and dealing damage to an opponent with their red X spells.

Fast Creature Decks

The simplest decks in Magic are the Fast Creature decks. There are two different types of Fast Creature decks. There are the Large Fast Creature decks that use a large amount of fast mana to generate a single threat, and there are the more common Small Fast Creature decks which spread out their roads to victory among a hoard of weaker creatures.

Large Fast Creature Decks

Fast Creature decks are perhaps the most common type of action based decks. The first variety of Fast Creature decks is Large Creature decks. These decks invest heavily in cards in order to bring out one large and durable creature. These decks, like most decks that work under fast deck theory, tend to lose speed after the first five rounds. They tend to run out of cards for their hand and can only generate one threat per turn at best. Players of Large Fast Creature decks hope that their advantage is large enough at that point that their opponent cannot effectively recover.

Cards that Work Well in Large Fast Creature Decks

Artifacts	Land	Red
1. Jeweled Amulet	1. Strip Mine	1. Orgg
2. Mana Vault		
3. Soldevi Simulacrum		

White	Blue	Black
1. Serra Angel	1. Air Elemental	1. Dark Ritual
2. Swords to Plowshares	2. Mahamoti Djinn	2. Derelore
		3. Vampire

Green
1. Ernham Djinn

The major weakness behind these decks is their poor card count economy. They frequently use two or three cards to deploy one active card. If these cards (the large creatures) disappear into the graveyard, then the deck loses its effectiveness, since three cards vanish with one blow. Cards like Unsummon, Swords to Plowshares, and Paralyze seriously harm these decks. For example, let us say you play a Swamp followed by a Dark Ritual, Mana Vault, and then a Vampire on the first turn. If your opponent responds by casting a Paralyze on your Vampire, he effectively counters three of your cards and one of your turns with one card. Your first turn melts away along with the Mana Vault, Dark Ritual, and Vampire.

Deck Name: FBD Type II: Large Fast Creature

Block One	Block Two	Block Three
Pocket 1	Pocket 1	Pocket 1
Ernham Djinn	Strip Mine	Swamp
Ernham Djinn	Strip Mine	Swamp
Ernham Djinn	Strip Mine	Swamp
Ernham Djinn	Strip Mine	Swamp
Pocket 2	Pocket 2	Pocket 2
Serra Angel	Barbed Sextant	Swamp
Serra Angel	Barbed Sextant	Swamp
Serra Angel	Barbed Sextant	Swamp

Serra Angel	Barbed Sextant	Swamp
Pocket 3	Pocket 3	Pocket 3
Vampire	Mana Vault	City of Brass
Vampire	Mana Vault	City of Brass
Vampire	Mana Vault	City of Brass
Vampire	Mana Vault	Brushland
Pocket 4	Pocket 4	Pocket 4
Savannah Lions	Dark Ritual	Brushland
Savannah Lions	Dark Ritual	Brushland
Savannah Lions	Dark Ritual	Brushland
Savannah Lions	Dark Ritual	Plains
Pocket 5	Pocket 5	Pocket 5
Derelore	Swords to Plowshares	Plains
Derelore	Swords to Plowshares	Plains
Disenchant	Swords to Plowshares	Plains
Disenchant	Swords to Plowshares	Plains

Sideboard:

1. Disenchant
2. Disenchant
3. Divine Offering
4. Divine Offering
5. Paralyze
6. Paralyze
7. Dark Banishing
8. Dark Banishing
9. Dark Banishing
10. C.O.P. Red
11. C.O.P. Red
12. C.O.P. Red
13. Pyroblast
14. Pyroblast
15. Pyroblast

Use Disenchants against Artifact decks, Paralyzes against Creature decks, C.O.P. Reds against Red decks, and Pyroblasts against Control Magic decks.

Small Fast Creature Decks

The second type of Fast Creature deck is the Small Fast Creature deck. This deck usually deploys multiple small creatures and spreads its investment out. Like Large Fast Creature decks, Small Fast Creature decks commonly lose momentum after the first five rounds. Overcoming this is the major challenge for fast creature players. Once a small creature player drops his hand, he has his entire investment in play. Cards that invoke mass permanent removal or creature removal can consume Small Fast Creature decks whole. For instance, if you have a number of small creatures in play and your opponent plays an Earthquake, he can effectively eliminate multiples of your cards with a single card. Once again, when these decks face opposing decks with the right cards, they tend to suffer immensely. If you apply attrition tactics and play one card a turn, you can overcome this obstacle.

These decks deal well against Counterspell decks, Land Destruction, and other decks that take time to develop before they can establish dominance. Cards that damage or stop Small Fast Creature decks are Earthquake, Hurricane, Nevinyrral's Disk, Wrath of God, Pyroclasym, and Balance.

Deck Name: FBD Type II: Fast Creature II

Block One	Block Two	Block Three
Pocket 1	Pocket 1	Pocket 1
Savannah Lions	Icatian Priests	Disenchant
Savannah Lions	Icatian Priests	Disenchant
Savannah Lions	Icatian Priests	Adarkar Wastes
Savannah Lions	Icatian Priests	Adarkar Wastes
Pocket 2	Pocket 2	Pocket 2
Benalish Hero	Kjeldoran Warrior	Adarkar Wastes
Benalish Hero	Kjeldoran Warrior	Adarkar Wastes
Benalish Hero	Kjeldoran Warrior	City of Brass
Benalish Hero	Kjeldoran Warrior	Plains
Pocket 3	Pocket 3	Pocket 3
Icatian Infantry	Crusade	Plains
Icatian Infantry	Crusade	Plains
Icatian Infantry	Crusade	Plains
Icatian Infantry	Crusade	Plains
Pocket 4	Pocket 4	Pocket 4
Icatian Javelineers	Howling Mine	Plains
Icatian Javelineers	Howling Mine	Plains
Icatian Javelineers	Howling Mine	Plains
Icatian Javelineers	Barbed Sextant	Plains
Pocket 5	Pocket 5	Pocket 5
Order of the White Shield	Swords to Plowshares	Plains

Order of the White Shield	Swords to Plowshares	Plains
Order of the White Shield	Swords to Plowshares	Plains
Order of the White Shield	Swords to Plowshares	Plains

Sideboard:

1. Disenchant
2. Disenchant
3. Eye for an Eye
4. Eye for an Eye
5. Eye for an Eye
6. Eye for an Eye
7. Armageddon
8. Armageddon
9. Sleight of Mind
10. Sleight of Mind
11. Sleight of Mind
12. Karma
13. Karma
14. Karma
15. Plains

This deck is cut to execute as quickly as possible without a use of elaborate card combinations. Most of the creatures cost only one white mana. This allows them to deploy quickly so they can inflict a large amount of damage before an opponent can deploy adequate defenses. After turns pass, the Priests take a more active role. They use excess mana to increase the size of other creatures. The Howling Mines are obviously there to reduce the loss of momentum. The Adarkar Wastes, City of Brass, and Barbed Sextant are present to overcome Gloom if you require the Sleights from the sideboard.

Hand Destruction

In Type II, Hand Destruction is one of the most ubiquitous of the powerful decks. There is little or no adequate defense available against Hand Destruction in Type II, with the exceptions of Counterspells and playing your cards as you draw them. Type I at least offers the Psychic Purge. If a player uses the Purge in an action-based deck, it can devastate a Hand Destruction deck. The banning of the Mind Twist harmed these decks but far from overwhelmed them.

Deck Name: FBD Hand Destruction (created by Jason Lee)

Block One	Block Two	Block Three
Pocket 1	Pocket 1	Pocket 1
Rack	Disrupting Scepter	Sulfurous Springs
Rack	Ihsan's Shade	Sulfurous Springs
Rack	Fireball	Sulfurous Springs
Rack	Fireball	Sulfurous Springs
Pocket 2	Pocket 2	Pocket 2
Hymn to Tourach	Lightning Bolt	City of Brass
Hymn to Tourach	Lightning Bolt	Swamp
Hymn to Tourach	Lightning Bolt	Swamp
Hymn to Tourach	Lightning Bolt	Swamp
Pocket 3	Pocket 3	Pocket 3
Hypnotic Specter	Dark Ritual	Swamp
Hypnotic Specter	Dark Ritual	Swamp
Hypnotic Specter	Dark Ritual	Swamp
Hypnotic Specter	Dark Ritual	Swamp
Pocket 4	Pocket 4	Pocket 4
Mindstab Thrull	Knights of Stromgald	Swamp
Mindstab Thrull	Knights of Stromgald	Swamp
Mindstab Thrull	Knights of Stromgald	Swamp
Mindstab Thrull	Knights of Stromgald	Swamp
Pocket 5	Pocket 5	Pocket 5
Vampire	Barbed Sextant	Mishra's Factory
Vampire	Barbed Sextant	Mishra's Factory
Vampire	Barbed Sextant	Mishra's Factory
Vampire	Barbed Sextant	Mishra's Factory

Sideboard:

1. Gloom	6. Shatter	11. Dark Banishing
2. Gloom	7. Shatter	12. Pyroblast
3. Gloom	8. Shatter	13. Pyroblast
4. Gloom	9. Dark Banishing	14. Pyroblast
5. Shatter	10. Dark Banishing	15. Pyroblast

Use Glooms against White decks, Shatters against Artifact decks, Dark Banishings against Large Creature decks, and Pyroblasts against Blue-based decks.

Jason Lee, one of the best players in Dallas, achieved a long winning streak with this deck in the winter of 1995. This interpretation of a Hand Destruction deck is not only a Tier One deck, but a solid Tier One deck. If you use this deck to test your deck against Hand Destruction and fare well, then your deck has no problems with Hand Destruction.

This deck, like all of the five basic decks, bases itself on the rather elementary concept of removing cards from an opponent's hand, causing him to suffer Rack damage. The lovely aspect of the Racks is that once hand destruction reduces a hand to no cards, a player requires three turns and six points of damage without playing any cards to get above a single Rack. This combination annihilates.

The most threatening deck type in Type II for a Hand Destruction deck remains the Counterspell deck. Sometimes, Counterspell decks fare relatively well against Hand Destruction decks, but this depends on each player's draw. Often Counterspell decks include no way to deal with a Mindstab Thrull or a Hypnotic Specter on the first turn. Once the Counterspell deck loses the battle for card count economy, the Hand Destruction deck dominates the Counterspell deck from that point on.

Chapter 15:

Miscellaneous Tournament Decks

This chapter is a collection of decks that don't really fit in any of the other sections of the book. They are all really good decks and deserve consideration. A diverse player should familiarize himself with and understand as many facets of his playing environment as he possibly can. Studying these decks should help better your playing skills and prepare you to face similar creations in the future.

Deck Name: Adam Maysonet's Green Plague

Block One	Block Two	Block Three
Pocket 1	Pocket 1	Pocket 1
Lhurgoyf	Force of Nature	Forest
Lhurgoyf	Autumn Willow	Forest
Lhurgoyf	Autumn Willow	Forest
Zuran Orb	Autumn Willow	Forest
Pocket 2	Pocket 2	Pocket 2
Ernham Djinn	Jayemdae Tome	Forest
Ernham Djinn	Jayemdae Tome	Forest
Ernham Djinn	Jayemdae Tome	Forest

Ernham Djinn	Forgotten Lore	Forest
Pocket 3	Pocket 3	Pocket 3
Llanowar Elves	Johtull Wurm	Forest
Llanowar Elves	Johtull Wurm	Forest
Llanowar Elves	Winter Blast	Forest
Llanowar Elves	Hurricane	Forest
Pocket 4	Pocket 4	Pocket 4
Fyndhorn Elves	Thelonite Druid	Forest
Fyndhorn Elves	Thelonite Druid	Forest
Fyndhorn Elves	Killer Bees	Forest
Fyndhorn Elves	Killer Bees	Forest
Pocket 5	Pocket 5	Pocket 5
Birds of Paradise	Cockatrice	Forest
Birds of Paradise	Cockatrice	Forest
Icy Manipulator	Forest	Forest
Icy Manipulator	Forest	Forest

Sideboard:

1. Primal Order
2. Primal Order
3. Crumble
4. Crumble
5. Crumble
6. Essence Filter
7. Essence Filter
8. Titania's Song
9. Winter Orb
10. Winter Orb
11. Ice Floe
12. Ice Floe
13. Aeolipile
14. Aeolipile
15. Aeolipile

Green Plague contains twenty-nine creatures which come out fast and furious. The Sideboard will handle most problems. The Winter Orbs shut down Direct Damage decks, and Ice Floes will damage big fast creature decks. Adam originally cut this for multi-player games but found it very competitive for duels.

Deck Name: The Land Tax, Land's Edge Deck

Block One	Block Two	Block Three
Pocket 1	Pocket 1	Pocket 1
Land Tax	Savannah Lions	Mishra's Factory
Land Tax	Savannah Lions	Mishra's Factory
Land Tax	Savannah Lions	City of Brass

Zuran Orb	Savannah Lions	City of Brass
Pocket 2	Pocket 2	Pocket 2
Land's Edge	Brassclaw Orcs	City of Brass
Land's Edge	Brassclaw Orcs	Plains
Land's Edge	Brassclaw Orcs	Plains
Balance	Brassclaw Orcs	Plains
Pocket 3	Pocket 3	Pocket 3
Lightning Bolt	Dwarven Soldier	Plains
Lightning Bolt	Dwarven Soldier	Plains
Lightning Bolt	Dwarven Soldier	Plains
Lightning Bolt	Dwarven Soldier	Plains
Pocket 4	Pocket 4	Pocket 4
Incinerate	Swords to Plowshares	Mountain
Incinerate	Swords to Plowshares	Mountain
Incinerate	Swords to Plowshares	Mountain
Incinerate	Swords to Plowshares	Mountain
Pocket 5	Pocket 5	Pocket 5
Disenchant	Strip Mine	Mountain
Disenchant	Strip Mine	Mountain
Strip Mine	Mishra's Factory	Mountain
Strip Mine	Mishra's Factory	Mountain

Sideboard:

1. Pyroblast	6. Disenchant	11. C.O.P. Red
2. Pyroblast	7. Divine Offering	12. Karma
3. Pyroblast	8. Divine Offering	13. Winter Orb
4. Pyroblast	9. C.O.P. Red	14. Winter Orb
5. Disenchant	10. C.O.P. Red	15. Winter Orb

Use Pyroblasts against Blue decks, Disenchants against Artifact decks, C.O.P. Reds against Burn decks, Karma against Black decks, and Winter Orbs against decks with expensive spells.

This deck is one example of the common Land's Edge/Land Tax deck. The deck never needs more than three lands to function so you can hold lands until you draw a Land Tax or a Land's Edge. The damage from the Land's Edge supplements the creature damage that an opponent will absorb from this deck's small creature hoard.

Deck Name: Degenerate de jour by Chris Pantages

Block One	Block Two	Block Three
Pocket 1	Pocket 1	Pocket 1
Derelore	Disenchant	Brushland
Derelore	Disenchant	Brushland
Derelore	Jayemdae Tome	Mountain
Derelore	Jayemdae Tome	Mountain
Pocket 2	Pocket 2	Pocket 2
Hymn to Tourach	Lightning Bolt	Sulfurous Springs
Hymn to Tourach	Lightning Bolt	Sulfurous Springs
Hymn to Tourach	Lightning Bolt	Mountain
Hymn to Tourach	Lightning Bolt	Mountain
Pocket 3	Pocket 3	Pocket 3
Dark Banishing	Balance	Forest
Dark Banishing	Fireball	Forest
Dark Banishing	Fireball	Forest
Dance of the Dead	Fireball	Forest
Pocket 4	Pocket 4	Pocket 4
Ernham Djinn	Dark Ritual	Forest
Ernham Djinn	Dark Ritual	Swamp
Ernham Djinn	Dark Ritual	Swamp
Ernham Djinn	Dark Ritual	Swamp
Pocket 5	Pocket 5	Pocket 5
Autumn Willow	City of Brass	Swamp
Autumn Willow	City of Brass	Swamp
Elvish Archer	City of Brass	Swamp
Elvish Archer	Karplusan Forest	Swamp

Sideboard:

1. Pyroblast
2. Pyroblast
3. Pyroblast
4. Pyroblast
5. Tranquility
6. Tranquility
7. Disenchant
8. Shatter
9. Shatter
10. Shatter
11. Order of the Ebon Hand
12. Knights of Stromgald
13. Knights of Stromgald
14. Knights of Stromgald
15. Knights of Stromgald

Use Pyroblasts against Blue Control decks, Tranquilities against Karma, Disenchant against Artifact heavy decks, and Order of the Ebon Hand against White Weenie decks.

Chris Pantages contructed this deck after reading through *The Duelist* and noticing some of the degenerate themes in the decks there. Inspired, he put together the most degenerate deck he could muster. One should take note of how Chris' mana producers are diversified, allowing him to effectively use four colors.

Deck Name: Lonnie Meador's Animate Deck

Block One	Block Two	Block Three
Pocket 1	Pocket 1	Pocket 1
Animate Dead	Incinerate	Sulfurous Springs
Animate Dead	Incinerate	Mountain
Animate Dead	Incinerate	Mountain
Animate Dead	Incinerate	Mountain
Pocket 2	Pocket 2	Pocket 2
Ball Lightning	Nevinyrral's Disk	Mountain
Ball Lightning	Nevinyrral's Disk	Mountain
Ball Lightning	Nevinyrral's Disk	Mountain
Shivan Dragon	Nevinyrral's Disk	Mountain
Pocket 3	Pocket 3	Pocket 3
Ihsan's Shade	Shatter	Mountain
Orgg	Safe Haven	Mountain
Mountain Yeti	Safe Haven	Mountain
Mountain Yeti	Zuran Orb	Swamp
Pocket 4	Pocket 4	Pocket 4
Vampire	Hymn to Tourach	Swamp
Eron the Relentless	Hymn to Tourach	Swamp
Fireball	Hymn to Tourach	Swamp
Fireball	Hymn to Tourach	Swamp
Pocket 5	Pocket 5	Pocket 5
Lightning Bolt	Jokulhaups	Swamp
Lightning Bolt	Sulfurous Springs	Swamp
Lightning Bolt	Sulfurous Springs	Swamp
Lightning Bolt	Sulfurous Springs	Swamp

Sideboard:

1. Simulacrum	6. Anarchy	11. Rack
2. Simulacrum	7. Anarchy	12. Rack
3. Simulacrum	8. Flashfires	13. Rack
4. Simulacrum	9. Gloom	14. Shatter
5. Anarchy	10. Rack	15. Shatter

Use Simulcrum against Burn decks, Anarchy against White decks, Rack against Fast decks, and Shatter against Artifact intensive decks.

Lonnie Meador is one of the more creative players in the South. This deck revolves mainly around the Animate Dead and Ball Lightning. When used in conjunction with the Safe Haven, Lonnie's deck brutally abuses other decks. Lonnie's unique mixture of damage sources provides him a diverse number of roads to victory.

Chapter 16:

Conclusion

Magic is not a game of pure strategy. There is a great deal of luck involved. The goal of a good Magic player is to always reduce the amount of luck and randomness involved in the game. We always strive to become more attuned to the great diversity of decks that exist in the grand Metagame of Type II. Magic resembles a giant game of rock, scissors, paper. Every deck has a weakness and will lose to some other deck. The trick is to find the deck with the fewest weaknesses, and then to master it so you can play it to its full potential.

The way strong Magic players face the game is similar to the way we deal with life. We do not have control of all of the random factors that take place from day to day, but we try to make do with the cards we are dealt (pardon the pun). We work to accumulate information and study those we believe successful. There is luck. There is always luck. But the harder you work towards understanding the game, the more likely it is you will be able to take advantage of your good fortune.

George Baxter
GBAXTER@ONRAMP.NET

Appendix A:

The Type II Banned and Restricted List, and Optional Rule

The Banned List

1. Amulet of Quoz
2. Ancestral Recall
3. Atog
4. Badlands
5. Basalt Monolith
6. Bayou
7. Berserk
8. Black Lotus
9. Blaze of Glory
10. Braingeyser
11. Bronze Tablet
12. Camouflauge
13. Chaos Orb
14. Channel
15. Clone
16. Consecrate Land
17. Contract from Below
18. Copper Tablet
19. Copy Artifact
20. Cyclopean Tomb
21. Darkpact
22. Demonic Attorney
23. Demonic Hordes
24. Demonic Tutor
25. Dwarven Demolition Team
26. Dwarven Weaponsmith
27. Earthbind
28. False Orders
29. Falling Star
30. Farmstead
31. Fastbond
32. Forcefield
33. Fork
34. Gauntlet of Might
35. Granite Gargoyle
36. Guardian Angel
37. Ice Storm
38. Illusionary Mask
39. Invisibility
40. Jade Statue
41. Jandor's Ring
42. Juggernaut

43. Kird Ape
44. Kudzu
45. Lance
46. Lich
47. Living Wall
48. Mijae Djinn
49. Mind Twist
50. Mox Emerald
51. Mox Jet
52. Mox Pearl
53. Mox Ruby
54. Mox Sapphire
55. Natural Selection
56. Nettling Imp
57. Plateau
58. Psionic Blast
59. Raging River
60. Rebirth
61. Reconstruction
62. Regrowth
63. Reconstruction
64. Reverse Polarity
65. Roc of Kher Ridges
66. Rock Hydra
67. Rocket Launcher
68. Sacrifice
69. Savannah
70. Scrubland
71. Sedge Troll
72. Serendib Efreet
73. Shatterstorm
74. Sinkhole
75. Sol Ring
76. Taiga
77. Tempest Efreet
78. Time Vault
79. Time Walk
80. Timetwister
81. Timmerian Fiends
82. Tropical Island
83. Tundra
84. Two-Headed Giant of Foriys
85. Underground Sea
86. Vesuvian Doppelganger
87. Veteran Bodyguard
88. Volcanic Island
89. Wheel of Fortune
90. Word of Command

Type II Restricted List

1. Balance
2. Black Vise
3. Feldon's Cane
4. Ivory Tower
5. Recall
6. Zuran Orb

Optional Rule

Whoever goes first skips the initial draw phase. The winner of the coin toss decides whether to draw first or play first. The loser of each successive duel decides whether he or she would like to play first or draw first.

Appendix B:

Complete List of All Type II Cards and Spoiler

Card	Type	Cost	P/T	Description
Abbey Gargoyles	Summon Gargoyles	WWW2	3/4	Protection from red, flying.
Abbey Matron	Summon Cleric	W2	1/3	W and Tap: Add +0/+3 to Matron until end of turn.
Abomination	Summon Abomination	BB3	2/6	Any green or white creature blocked by or blocking it is destroyed at the end of combat.
Abu Ja 'far	Summon Leper	W	0/1	If destroyed in combat, all creatures blocked by or blocking it are destroyed.
Abyssal Specter	Summon Specter	BB2	2/3	Flying. Whenever it damages a player, that player must discard a card of his choice.
Active Volcano	Instant	R	--	Destroy blue permanent or return 1 island in play to its owner's hand.
Adarkar Sentinel	Artifact Creature	5	3/3	1: +0/+1 bonus to toughness until end of turn.
Adarkar Unicorn	Summon Unicorn	WW1	2/2	Tap to add U or U1 to your mana pool which is only usable to pay cumulative upkeep. Play this ability as an interrupt.

Card	Type	Cost	P/T	Description
Adarkar Wastes	Land	--	--	Tap to add 1 colorless to your mana pool or tap to add W to your mana pool and suffer 1 damage or tap to add U to your mana pool and suffer 1 damage.
Aegis of the Meek	Artifact	3	--	Tap+(1) Target 1/1 creature gains +1/+2.
Aeolipile	Artifact	2	--	Tap+(1) Sacrifice to do 2 damage to any target.
Aether Storm	Enchantment	U3	--	Summon spells may no longer be cast. Any player may pay 4 life to bury Aether Storm. Effects that redirect or prevent this damage cannot be used to counter this loss of life.
Aggression	Enchant Creature	R2	--	Target non-wall creature in play gains first strike and trample abilities. At the end of its controller's turn destroy if it did not attack that turn.
Air Elemental	Summon Elemental	UU3	4/4	Flying.
Akron Legionnaire	Summon Legionnaire	WW6	8/4	None of your non-artifact creatures may attack except Legionnaires.
Alabaster Potion	Instant	WWX	--	Gain X life or prevent X damage to one target.
Aladdin	Summon Aladdin	RR2	1/1	RR1: Steal artifact.
Aladdin's Lamp	Artifact	10	--	Tap+(X) Instead of drawing a card during your draw phase draw X cards during upkeep and keep only one.
Aladdin's Ring	Artifact	8	--	Tap+(8) Do 4 damage to any target.
Ali Baba	Summon Ali Baba	R	1/1	Tap+(R) Tap a wall.
Aliban's Tower	Instant	R1	--	Target blocking creature gains +3/+1 until the end of the turn.
Altar of Bone	Sorcery	WG	--	Sacrifice a creature to look through your library and get a creature into you hand after showing it to all players.
Ambush	Instant	R3	--	All Blocking Creatures gain first strike until the end of turn.
Ambush Party	Summon Ambush Party	R4		May attack on the turn it comes into play. First strike.
Amrou Kithkin	Summon Kithkin	WW	1/1	Cannot be blocked by creatures with a power greater than 2.

Card	Type	Cost	P/T	Description
Amulet of Kroog	Artifact	2	--	Tap+(2) Prevent 1 damage to any target.
Amulet of Quoz	Artifact	6	--	Use only if playing for ante. Tap+(0): Sacrifice Amulet of Quoz and flip a coin. Your favor: opponent loses. Opponent's favor: you lose. Opponent can ante another card to counter this effect.
An-Havva Constable	Summon Constable	GG1	2/1+*	The Constable has toughness equal to one plus the total number of green creatures in play.
An-Havva Inn	Sorcery	GG1	--	Gain 1+* life, where * is equal to the total number of green creatures in play.
An-Havva Township	Land	--	--	Tap to add one colorless mana to your mana pool. Tap and pay one colorless to add one G to your mana pool. Tap and pay two and add one W or one R to your mana pool.
An-Zerrin Ruins	Enchantment	RR2	--	You must choose a creature type when cast. Creatures of that type do not untap during their untap phase.
Anaba Ancestor	Summon Ghost	R1	1/1	Tap to give target Minotaur +1/+1 until the end of the turn.
Anaba Bodyguard	Summon Bodyguard	R3	2/3	First strike.
Anaba Shaman	Summon Minotaur	R3	2/2	R and tap to deal one damage to target creature or player.
Anaba Spirit Crafter	Summon Minotaur	RR2	1/3	Spirit Crafter gives all Minotaurs +1/+0.
Anarchy	Sorcery	RR2	--	Destroy all white permanents in play when cast.
Angelic Voices	Enchantment	WW2	--	+1/+1 to all your creatures as long as they are all white or artifact creatures.
Angry Mob	Summon Mob	WW2	2+*/2+*	Trample. During your turn, the *'s are equal to the number of swamps all opponents control.
Animate Artifact	Enchant Artifact	U3	--	Makes a target artifact a */* artifact creature where * is the casting cost of the artifact.
Animate Dead	Enchant Dead Creature	B1	--	Return 1 creature from any graveyard to play under your control at -1 power.
Animate Wall	Enchant Wall	W	--	Target wall can now attack.

Card	Type	Cost	P/T	Description
Ankh of Mishra	Artifact	2	--	Any time any player brings a land into play, does 2 points of damage to that player.
Apocalypse Chime	Artifact	2	--	Two and tap: Sacrifice Chime to bury all Homelands cards.
Apprentice Wizard	Summon Wizard	UU1	0/1	Tap+(U) add 3 to your mana pool.
Arcades Sabboth	Summon Elder Dragon Legend	UUGG WW2	7/7	Flying. (W):+0/+1. Your untapped and not attacking creatures gain +0/+2. Pay UGW during your upkeep or this card is buried.
Arctic Foxes	Summon Foxes	W1	1/1	If defending player controls no snow-covered lands
Arcum's Sleigh	Artifact	1	--	Tap+(2) Attacking this turn does not cause target creature to tap. You may not use this ability if defending player has no snow-covered lands in play.
Arcum's Weathervane	Artifact	2	--	Tap+(2) Make a snow-covered land non-snow-covered or vice versa. Mark this change with a counter.
Arcum's Whistle	Artifact	3	--	Tap+(3) Target non-wall creature must attack. At end of turn, destroy if it was unable attack. Use this ability only during the creature controller's turn before he or she declares an attack. The creature's controller may counter by paying the creature's casting cost. Does not affect creatures brought into play that turn.
Arena of the Ancients	Artifact	3	--	Taps all legends as they enter play, legends do not untap as normal.
Arenson's Aura	Enchantment	W2	--	W: Sacrifice an enchantment to destroy target enchantment in play. UU3: Counter target enchantment as it is cast.
Argothian Pixies	Summon Faeries	G1	2/1	Cannot be blocked by artifact creatures. Ignores damage from artifact sources.
Armageddon	Sorcery	W3	--	Destroys all lands in play.
Armageddon Clock	Artifact	6	--	Add 1 counter each upkeep. Does 1 damage to each player for each counter at end of upkeep. Any player may remove a counter during upkeep for 4 mana.

Card	Type	Cost	P/T	Description
Armor of Faith	Enchant Creature	W	--	Target creature gets +1/+1. W: Enchanted creature gets +0/+1 until end of turn.
Armor Thrull	Summon Thrull	B2	1/3	Tap and sacrifice to add a +1/+2 counter to target creature.
Arnjlot's Ascent	Enchantment	UU1	--	Cumulative upkeep: U. 1: Target creature in play gains flying ability until end of turn.
Ashen Ghoul	Summon Ghoul	B3	3/1	Can attack the turn it comes into play. B: Return to play under your control. Use this ability only at the end of your upkeep and only if it is in your graveyard with 3 creatures above it.
Ashes to Ashes	Sorcery	BB1	--	Removes 2 target non-artifact creatures from the game and does 5 damage to caster.
Ashnod's Altar	Artifact	3	--	0: Sacrifice a creature to gain 2 colorless mana.
Ashnod's Battle Gear	Artifact	2	--	Tap+(2) Give creature +2/-2. Effect remains until untapped. May choose not to untap.
Ashnod's Transmogrant	Artifact	1	--	Sacrifice Transmogrant to give any creature +1/+1 and make it an artifact creature.
Aspect of Wolf	Enchant Creature	G1	--	Gives +*/+* where * is 1/2 number of forests.
Aurochs	Summon Aurochs	G3	2/3	Trample. When attacking, gets a +1/+0 bonus for each of the other Aurochs that attack.
Autumn Willow	Summon Legend	GG4	4/4	Cannot be the target of spells or effects. G: Target player may target Willow with effects and spells until the end of the turn.
Avalanche	Sorcery	RR2X	--	Destroy X snow-covered lands in play.
Axelrod Gunnarson	Summon Legend	BBRR4	5/5	Trample. Gives you 1 life and does 1 damage to opponent when a creature goes to the graveyard on a turn in which Axelrod damages.
Ayesha Tanaka	Summon Legend	UUWW	2/2	Banding. Tap to counter effect of an artifact with an activation cost unless opponent pays W.

Card	Type	Cost	P/T	Description
Aysen Abbey	Land	--	--	Tap to add one colorless mana to your mana pool. Tap and pay one colorless to add one W to your mana pool. Tap and pay two and add one U or one G to your mana pool.
Aysen Bureaucrats	Summon Bureaucrats	W1	1/1	Tap: Tap target creature of controller's choice with power no greater than 2.
Aysen Crusader	Summon Crusader	WW2	2+*/2+*	* is equal to the number of Heroes you control.
Aysen Highway	Enchantment	WWW3		All white creatures now have plainswalk.
Azure Drake	Summon Drake	U3	2/4	Flying.
Backfire	Enchant Creature	U	--	For each point of damage done to you by target creature, Backfire does 1 point of damage to target's controller.
Bad Moon	Enchantment	B1	--	All black creatures in play get +1/+1.
Baki's Curse	Sorcery	UU2	--	Deals two damage to each creature for each creature enchantment on that creature.
Balance	Sorcery	W1	--	Balance number of creatures, lands, and cards in hand.
Balduvian Barbarians	Summon Barbarians	RR1	3/2	
Balduvian Bears	Summon Bears	G1	2/2	
Balduvian Conjurer	Summon Wizard	U1	0/2	Tap to turn target snow-covered land into a 2/2 creature. Cannot be tapped for mana if it came into play this turn.
Balduvian Hydra	Summon Hydra	RRX	0/1	When comes into play put X +1/+0 counters on it. 0: Remove a counter to prevent 1 damage to it. RRR: Put a counter on it that is only usable during your upkeep.
Balduvian Shaman	Summon Cleric	U	1/1	Tap to permanently change the text of target white enchantment you control that does not have cumulative upkeep by replacing all instances of one color with another.
Ball Lightning	Summon Ball Lightning	RRR	6/1	Trample. Can attack on turn it comes into play. Is buried at end of turn it comes into play.

Card	Type	Cost	P/T	Description
Balm of Restoration	Artifact	2	--	Tap+(1) Sacrifice to gain 2 life or prevent 2 damage to any player or creature.
Banshee	Summon Banshee	BB2	0/1	Tap+(X) Banshee does X damage, half (rounded up) to you and half (rounded down) to your opponent.
Barbarian Guides	Summon Barbarians	B2	1/2	Tap+(R2): Target creature you control gains a snow-covered landwalk ability until end of turn. Return that creature to owner's hand from play at end of turn.
Barbed Sextant	Artifact	1	--	Tap+(1) Sacrifice to add 1 mana of any color to your pool and play as an interrupt. Draw a card at the beginning of the next turn's upkeep.
Barl's Cage	Artifact	4	--	3: Target creature does not untap as normal during its controller's next untap phase.
Baron Sengir	Summon Legend	BBB5	5/5	Flying. When a creature is put into the graveyard the same turn that the Baron damaged it, add a +2+2 counter to the Banon. Tap to regenerate target Vampire.
Basal Thrull	Summon Thrull	BB	1/2	Tap and sacrifice to add BB to your mana pool.
Baton of Morale	Artifact	2	--	2: Target creature gains banding ability until the end of the turn.
Battering Ram	Artifact Creature	2	1/1	Bands only when attacking. Destroys blocking walls.
Battle Cry	Instant	W2	--	Untap all white creatures in play you control. Any creature that blocks this turn gets a +0/+1 bonus to its toughness until end of the turn.
Battle Frenzy	Instant	R2	--	All green creatures you control get +1/+1 and non-green get +1/+0 until end of turn.
Beast Walkers	Summon Heroes	WW1	2/2	G: Gains banding until the end of turn.
Beasts of Bogardan	Summon Beasts	R4	3/3	Protection from red. Gain +1/+1 if opponent has white cards in play.
Benalish Hero	Summon Hero	W	1/1	Banding.
Bird Maiden	Summon Bird Maiden	R2	1/2	Flying.

Card	Type	Cost	P/T	Description
Birds of Paradise	Summon Mana Birds	G	0/1	Flying. Tap to add 1 mana of any color to your mana pool.
Binding Grasp	Enchantment	U3	--	Pay 1U during upkeep or bury Binding Grasp. Gain control of target creature, and it gains +0/+1.
Black Carriage	Summon Carriage	BB3	4/4	Trample. Does not untap duing the untap phase. 0: Sacrifice a creature during your upkeep to untap the Black Carriage.
Black Knight	Summon Knight	BB	2/2	Protection from white. First strike.
Black Mana Battery	Artifact	4	--	Tap+(2) add a token to Battery. Tap to add B to your mana pool. Also can convert tokens to B.
Black Scarab	Enchant Creature	W	--	Target creature gets +2/+2 as long as opponent controls any black cards and cannot be blocked by black cards.
Black Vise	Artifact	1	--	During your opponent's upkeep, does 1 damage to opponent for each card in their hand above 4.
Black Ward	Enchant Creature	W	--	Target creature gains protection from black.
Blessed Wine	Instant	W1	--	Gain 1 life. Draw a card from the library at the beginning of the next turn's upkeep phase.
Blessing	Enchant Creature	WW	--	W: Target creature gains +1/+1 until end of turn.
Blight	Enchant Land	BB	--	If land is tapped it is destroyed at end of turn.
Blinking Spirit	Summon Blinking Spirit	W3	2/2	0: Return Blinking Spirit from play to owner's hand.
Blizzard	Enchantment	GG	--	Cumulative upkeep: 2. Cannot cast if you don't control snow-covered land. Creatures with flying do not untap as normal.
Blood Lust	Instant	R1	--	Target creature gains +4/-4 until end of turn. If this reduces a creature's toughness below 1, its toughness is now 1.
Blood Moon	Enchantment	R2	--	All non-basic lands in play are now basic mountains.

Card	Type	Cost	P/T	Description
Blood of the Martyr	Instant	WWW	--	For the remainder of the turn you may redirect damage done to any of your creatures to yourself.
Blue Elemental Blast	Interrupt	U	--	Counters target red spell as it is being cast, or destroys target red card in play.
Blue Mana Battery	Artifact	4	--	Tap+(2) add a token to Battery. Tap to add U to your mana pool. Also can convert tokens to U.
Blue Scarab	Enchant Creature	W	--	Target creature gets +2/+2 as long as opponent controls any blue cards and cannot be blocked by blue creatures.
Blue Ward	Enchant Creature	W	--	Target creature gains protection from blue.
Bog Imp	Summon Imp	B1	1/1	Flying.
Bog Rats	Summon Rats	B	1/1	Cannot be blocked by walls.
Bog Wraith	Summon Wraith	B3	3/3	Swampwalk.
Bone Shaman	Summon Giant	RR2	3/3	B: Creature damaged by this creature cannot regenerate until end of turn.
Book of Raas	Artifact	6	--	2: Pay 2 life to draw one card. Damage may not be prevented or redirected.
Boomerang	Instant	UU	--	Return target permanent to owner's hand.
Bottle of Suleiman	Artifact	5	--	1: Sacrifice and flip a coin. If you win you get a 5/5 flying artifact creature; if you lose you take 5 damage.
Bottomless Vault	Land	--	--	Comes into play tapped. May leave tapped to add 1 storage counter. Tap and remove X storage counters to add X B to your mana pool.
Brainstorm	Instant	B	--	Draw 3 cards then take 2 from hand and place on top of your library.
Brainwash	Enchant Creature	W	--	Target creature cannot attack unless its controller pays 3 in addition to any other costs.
Brand of Ill Omen	Enchant Creature	R3	--	Cumulative upkeep: R. Target creature's controller cannot cast summons.
Brass Man	Artifact Creature	1	1/3	Does not untap as normal. Pay 1 to untap during your upkeep.
Brassclaw Orcs	Summon Orcs	R2	3/2	Cannot be assigned to block any creature of power greater than 1.

Card	Type	Cost	P/T	Description
Breath of Dreams	Enchantment	UU2	--	Cumulative upkeep: U. Green creatures in play each require an additional cumulative upkeep of 1 to remain in play.
Breeding Pit	Enchantment	B3	--	During your upkeep pay BB or is destroyed. At end of your turn bring a Thrull counter into play. Treat as 0/1 black creature.
Brine Shaman	Summon Cleric	B1	1/1	Tap and sacrifice a creature to give target creature +2/+2 bonus until end of turn. UU1: Sacrifice a creature in play to counter target summon spell when cast.
Broken Visage	Instant	B4	--	Bury target non-artifact ataking creature. Put a black Shadow token in play. Token has the same power and toughness as the targeted attacking creature. Bury token at end of turn.
Bronze Horse	Artifact Creature	7	4/4	Trample. Not damaged by targeted spells if you have other creatures in play.
Bronze Tablet	Artifact	6	--	Tap+(4) Swap Tablet w/any card in play. Effect is permanent but may be countered with a loss of 10 life. Ante games only.
Brothers of Fire	Summon Brothers	RR1	2/2	RR1: Brothers of Fire does 1 damage to any target and 1 damage to you.
Brown Ouphe	Summon Ouphe	G	1/1	Tap+(G1): Target artifact ability which requires an activation cost. Use as an interrupt.
Brushland	Land	--	--	Tap to add 1 colorless to your mana pool or tap to add W to your mana pool and suffer 1 damage or tap to add G to your mana pool and suffer 1 damage.
Brute, The	Enchant Creature	R1	--	Target creature gains +1/+0 and RRR: Regenerates.
Burnt Offering	Interrupt	B	--	Sacrifice a creature under your control to add its casting cost in any combination of red and black mana to your pool.
Burrowing	Enchant Creature	R	--	Target creature gains mountainwalk.

Card	Type	Cost	P/T	Description
Call to Arms	Enchantment	W1	--	Choose a color. As long as target opponent controls more cards of that color than any other, all white creatures in play get a +1/+1 bonus added to their power and toughness. If at any time that opponent does not control more cards of that color than any other, bury this card.
Carapace	Enchant Creature	G	--	Target creature gets +0/+2 and you may sacrifice Carapace to regenenerate the creature that Carapace is on.
Caribou Range	Enchant Land	WW2	--	WW: Tap land it enchants to put a 0/1 white Caribou token into play. 0: Sacrifice a Caribou token to gain 1 life.
Carnivorous Plant	Summon Wall	G3	4/5	Wall.
Carrion Ants	Summon Ants	BB2	0/1	1: +1/+1 until end of turn.
Castle	Enchantment	W3	--	All your untapped, non-attacking creatures gain +0/+2.
Castle Sengir	Land	--	--	Tap to add one colorless mana to your mana pool. Tap and pay one colorless to add one B to your mana pool. Tap and pay two and add one U or one R to your mana pool.
Cat Warriors	Summon Cat Warriors	GG1	2/2	Forestwalk.
Cave People	Summon Cave People	RR1	1/4	If declared as an attacker gains +1/-2 until end of turn. Tap+(RR1) Target creature gains mountainwalk until end of turn.
Celestial Prism	Artifact	3	--	Tap+(2) Add 1 mana of any color to your mana pool.
Celestial Sword	Artifact	6	--	Tap+(3) Target creature you control gets +3/+3 until the end of the turn, then bury that target creature.
Cemetery Gate	Summon Wall	B2	0/5	Protection from black.
Centaur Archer	Summon Centaur	RG1	3/2	Tap to deal 1 damage to target flying creature.
Chain Stasis	Instant	U	--	Tap or untap target creature. Whenever a player uses Chain Stasis to tap or untap a creature, the creature's controller can pay U2 to use the Chain Stasis to tap or untap any target creature.

Card	Type	Cost	P/T	Description
Chandler	Summon Legend	R4	3/3	Pay RRR and tap to destroy target artifact creature.
Channel	Sorcery	GG	--	Convert life into colorless mana until end of turn.
Chaos Lord	Summon Lord	RRR4	7/7	First strike. Can attack the turn it comes into play on a side. The exception for this is the turn it is cast. If during your upkeep, the number of permanents under controller's control is even, it switches to opponent's control.
Chaos Moon	Enchantment	R3	--	If number of permanents is odd all red creatures get +1/+1 and mountains produce an extra R until end of turn. If even all red creatures get -1/-1 and mountains produce colorless mana.
Chaoslace	Interrupt	R	--	Changes the color of one card in play to red.
Chromatic Armor	Enchant Creature	WU1	--	When played, put a sleight counter on it and choose a color. Any damage dealt to target by sources of that color is reduced to 0. X: Put a sleight counter on Armor and change the color that it protects again. X is the number of sleight counters on it.
Chromium	Summon Elder Dragon Legend	BBUU WW2	7/7	Flying. Rampage: 2. Pay BUW during your upkeep or this card is buried.
Chub Toad	Summon Toad	G2	1/1	Gets +2/+2 until end of turn when attacking or blocking.
Circle of Protection: Artifacts	Enchantment	W1	--	2: Reduce the damage done to you from one artifact source to zero.
Circle of Protection: Black	Enchantment	W1	--	1: Prevent damage done to you from one black source.
Circle of Protection: Blue	Enchantment	W1	--	1: Prevent damage done to you from one blue source.
Circle of Protection: Green	Enchantment	W1	--	1: Prevent damage done to you from one green source.
Circle of Protection: Red	Enchantment	W1	--	1: Prevent damage done to you from one red source.
Circle of Protection: White	Enchantment	W1	--	1: Prevent damage done to you from one white source.

Card	Type	Cost	P/T	Description
City of Brass	Land	--	--	Tap for 1 mana of any color. Take 1 damage whenever tapped.
Clairvoyance	Instant	U	--	Look at target player's hand. Draw a card from the library at the beginning of next turn's upkeep.
Clay Statue	Artifact Creature	4	3/1	2: Regenerates.
Cloak of Confusion	Enchant Creature	B1	--	If target creature you control that has Cloak of Confusion on it attacks and is not blocked you may choose to have the creature deal no damage and force an opponent to discard a card from his hand at random. This ability is ignored if target opponent has no cards in hand.
Clockwork Avian	Artifact Creature	5	0/4	Flying. Starts with 4 +1/+0 counters on it. Remove 1 counter whenever it attacks or defends. Can replace tokens during upkeep for 1 each but this taps the Avian.
Clockwork Beast	Artifact Creature	6	0/4	Starts with 7 +1/+0 counters on it. Remove 1 counter whenever it attacks or defends. Can replace tokens for 1 during upkeep but this taps the Beast.
Clockwork Gnomes	Artifact Creature	4	2/2	Pay three and tap to regenerate target artifact creature.
Clockwork Steed	Artifact Creature	4	0/3	Clockwork Steed cannot be blocked by artifact creatures. When Steed enters play place four +1/+0 counters on it. At the end of combat in which it attacked or blocked, remove a counter. X+T: Place X +1/+0 counters on Steed. You may not have more than 4 counters on it. Do this only during upkeep.
Clockwork Swarm	Artifact Creature	4	0/3	Clockwork Swarm cannot be blocked by walls. When Swarm enters play place four +1/+0 counters on it. At the end of any combat in which it attacked or blocked, remove a counter. X+T: Place X +1/+0 counters on Swarm. You man not have more than 4 counters on it. Do this only during upkeep.
Cockatrice	Summon Cockatrice	GG3	2/4	Flying. Any non-wall creatures blocking or blocked by Cockatrice are destroyed at end of combat.

Card	Type	Cost	P/T	Description
Cocoon	Enchant Creature	G	--	Taps creature and holds it tapped for three turns. Then it gets +1/+1 and flying.
Cold Snap	Enchantment	W2	--	Cumulative upkeep: 2. During each player's upkeep does 1 damage to that player for each snow-covered land he controls.
Colossus of Sardia	Artifact Creature	9	9/9	Trample. Does not untap as normal. Must pay 9 during your upkeep to untap.
Combat Medic	Summon Soldier	W2	0/2	W1: Prevent 1 damage to any player or creature.
Conch Horn	Artifact	2	--	Tap+(1) Sacrifice and draw 2 cards. Return any card from your hand to deck.
Concordant Crossroads	Enchant World	G	--	Creatures may attack on the turn in which they are summoned.
Conquer	Enchant Land	RR3	--	Gain control of target land.
Conservator	Artifact	4	--	Tap+(3) Prevent the loss of 2 life.
Control Magic	Enchant Creature	UU2	--	Take control of target creature.
Conversion	Enchantment	WW2	--	All mountains in play are considered plains. Controller must pay WW during upkeep or is destroyed.
Cooperation	Enchant Creature	W2	--	Target creature gains banding.
Coral Helm	Artifact	3	--	3: Give target creature +2/+2 until end of turn. When ability is used, you must randomly discard a card from your hand.
Coral Reef	Enchantment	UU		When Reef comes into play place four polyp counters on it. B: Tap target blue creature you control and remove a counter from Coral Reef to place a +0/+1 counter on any target creature. 0: Sacrifice an island to place two target counters on Reef.
Cosmic Horror	Summon Horror	BBB3	7/7	First strike. Pay BBB3 during upkeep or does 7 damage to you and is destroyed.
Counterspell	Interrupt	UU	--	Counters target spell.
Craw Giant	Summon Giant	GGG G3	6/4	Trample. Rampage: 2.
Craw Wurm	Summon Wurm	GG4	6/4	

Card	Type	Cost	P/T	Description
Creature Bond	Enchant Creature	U1	--	If target creature goes to the graveyard its controller takes damage equal to its toughness.
Crimson Manticore	Summon Manticore	RR2	2/2	Flying. Tap to do 1 damage to attacking or blocking creature.
Crown of the Ages	Artifact	2	--	Tap+(4) Switch target enchantment from one creature to another legal target. The controller does not change. Treat target enchantment as though it were just cast on the new target.
Crumble	Instant	G	--	Buries target artifact and gives controller life equal to its casting cost.
Crusade	Enchantment	WW	--	All white creatures in play gain +1/+1.
Crystal Rod	Artifact	1	--	1: Gain 1 life whenever a blue spell is cast.
Cuombajj Witches	Summon Witches	BB	1/3	Tap to do 1 damage to any target. Opponent also gets to do 1 damage to any target.
Curse of Marit Lage	Enchantment	RR3	--	When comes into play tap all islands in play. Islands no longer untap during controller's untap phase.
Cursed Land	Enchant Land	BB2	--	Does 1 damage to controller of target during his or her upkeep.
Cursed Rack	Artifact	4	--	Your opponent must discard down to 4 cards at the end of his or her discard phase.
Cyclone	Enchantment	GG2	--	Gets 1 token each upkeep. Must pay G for each token or is discarded. Does 1 damage per token to all players and creatures.
Cyclopean Mummy	Summon Mummy	B1	2/1	Is removed from the game when it goes to the graveyard from play.
D'Avenant Archer	Summon Archer	W2	1/2	Tap to do 1 damage to an attacking or blocking creature.
Dakkon Blackblade	Summon Legend	BUU W2	*/*	Where * is the number of lands you control.
Dance of Many	Enchantment	UU	--	Create a token copy of creature in play with all of its characteristics. Controller must pay UU during his or her upkeep or Dance of Many is buried. If Dance of Many leaves play, token creature is destroyed.

Card	Type	Cost	P/T	Description
Dance of the Dead	Enchant Dead Creature	B1	--	Take dead creature from any graveyard and place it in play under your control, tapped with a +1/+1 bonus and treated as if just summoned. That creature does not untap as normal. At the end of its controller's upkeep, may pay an additional B1 to untap that creature. If Dance of Dead is removed from target creature then it is placed in its owner's graveyard.
Dancing Scimitar	Artifact Creature	4	1/5	Flying.
Dandan	Summon Dandan	UU	4/1	Cannot attack if opponent does not have islands. Destroyed if you have no islands.
Dark Banishing	Instant	B2	--	Destroy target non-black creature without possibility of regenerating.
Dark Maze	Summon Wall	U4	4/5	0: Dark Maze can attack this turn. At the end of the turn remove the Maze from the game. The Maze cannot attack on the turn it comes into play.
Dark Ritual	Interrupt	B	--	Add BBB to your mana pool.
Daughter of Autumn	Summon Legend	GG2	2/4	W: Redirect to Daughter of Autumn one damage taken by a white creature.
Death Speakers	Summon Speakers	W	1/1	Protection from black.
Death Ward	Instant	W	--	Regenerates target creature.
Deathgrip	Enchantment	BB	--	BB: Counters a green spell as it is being cast.
Deathlace	Interrupt	B	--	Changes color of target permanent to black.
Deep Spawn	Summon Homarid	UUU5	6/6	Trample. During your upkeep, take two cards from top of your library and put them in your graveyard or destroy Deep Spawn. U: Deep Spawn may not be the target of fast effects or spells until end of turn and does not untap as normal during your next upkeep phase. If Deep Spawn is untapped tap it.
Deflection	Interrupt	U3	--	Target spell with single target now targets a new target of your choice.

Card	Type	Cost	P/T	Description
Delif's Cone	Artifact	0	--	Tap and sacrifice this card. If creature you control attacks and is not blocked you may choose not to deal damage with this creature and gain life equal to its power.
Delif's Cube	Artifact	1	--	Tap+(2) If target creature you control attacks and is not blocked instead of doing damage you gain a cube counter. 2: Remove a token to regenerate target creature.
Demonic Consultation	Instant	B	--	Caster names a card and removes the top 6 cards of library. The next card is revealed. If the card is the card named it may be placed in its caster's hand; if not the card is removed from the game. This continues until the card named is revealed.
Derelor	Summon Thrull	B3	4/4	Your black spells cost an additional B to cast.
Desert Twister	Sorcery	GG4	--	Destroy any one card in play.
Despotic Scepter	Artifact	1	--	Tap to bury a target permanent you control.
Detonate	Sorcery	RX	--	Destroys an artifact without regeneration and does X damage to controller. X is casting cost of artifact.
Diabolic Machine	Artifact Creature	7	4/4	3: Regenerates.
Diabolic Vision	Sorcery	UB	--	Caster looks at the top 5 cards of his deck and puts 1 of them into his hand. The remaining 4 are placed on top of library in any order.
Didgeridoo	Artifact	1	--	3: Take a Minotaur from your hand and place it into play as though it were just summoned.
Dingus Egg	Artifact	4	--	When any land is destroyed controller takes 2 points of damage.
Dire Wolves	Summon Wolves	G2	2/2	Gains banding ability if you control any plains in play.
Disenchant	Instant	W1	--	Destroys target artifact or enchantment in play.
Disintegrate	Sorcery	RX	--	Does X damage to any 1 target. Target cannot regenerate. If dies this turn, leaves game.

Card	Type	Cost	P/T	Description
Disrupting Scepter	Artifact	3	--	Tap+(3) Opponent must discard a card of his or her choice. This may only be used during controller's turn.
Divine Offering	Instant	W1	--	Destroy target artifact and gain life equal to its casting cost.
Divine Transformation	Enchant Creature	WW2	--	Target creature gains +3/+3.
Draconian Cylix	Artifact	3	--	Tap+(2) Discard a card at random from your hand to regenerate target creature.
Dragon Engine	Artifact Creature	3	1/3	2: +1/+0 until end of turn.
Dragon Whelp	Summon Dragon	RR2	2/3	Flying. R: +1/+0 until end of turn. If more than RRR is spent in this way during one turn, Dragon Whelp is destroyed at end of turn.
Drain Life	Sorcery	B1	--	Does X damage to target and adds X to caster's life. X must be black mana.
Drain Power	Sorcery	UU	--	Tap all of opponent's land and add this mana to your mana pool.
Dread Wight	Summon Wight	BB3	3/4	Any creature that blocks or is blocked by Wight becomes tapped and gets a paralyzation counter. Creature does not untap if it has a counter on it. Target's controller can remove a counter as a fast effect for 4.
Dreams of the Dead	Enchantment	U3	--	U1: Take target white or black creature from your graveyard and put it directly into play as though it were just summoned. That creature now requires an additional cumulative upkeep: 2. If the creature leaves play, remove it from the game entirely.
Drift of the Dead	Summon Wall	B3	*/*	Where * is the number of snow-covered lands you control.
Drought	Enchantment	WW2	--	During your upkeep pay WW or it is destroyed. For each B in any spell or activation cost, caster or controller must sacrifice one swamp.
Drudge Skeletons	Summon Skeletons	B1	1/1	B: Regenerates.

Card	Type	Cost	P/T	Description
Drudge Spell	Enchantment	BB	--	B: Remove two creatures from your graveyard to put a 1/1 Skeleton token into play. Treat the token as a black creature with "B:regenerate." If Drudge Spell leaves play, bury all Skeleton tokens.
Dry Spell	Sorcery	B1	--	All players and creatures are dealt one point of damage by Dry Spell.
Durkwood Boars	Summon Boars	G4	4/4	
Dwarven Armorer	Summon Dwarf	R	0/2	Tap+(R) Discard a card from your hand to put either a +9/+1 or a +1/+0 counter on target creature.
Dwarven Armory	Enchantment	RR2	--	2: Sacrifice a land in play to put a +2/+2 bonus power and toughness counter on target creature. Use only during the upkeep phase.
Dwarven Catapult	Instant	RX	--	Does X damage divided evenly among opponent's creatures, rounded down.
Dwarven Hold	Land	--	--	Comes into play tapped. May leave tapped to add 1 storage counter. Tap and remove X storage counters to add X R to your mana pool.
Dwarven Lieutenant	Summon Dwarf	RR	2/1	R1: Target Dwarf gets +1/+0 until end of turn.
Dwarven Pony	Summon Pony	R	1/1	1R and Tap: Target Dwarf gains mountainwalk until the end of the turn.
Dwarven Ruins	Land	--	--	Comes into play tapped. Tap to add R to your mana pool. Tap and sacrifice to add RR to your mana pool.
Dwarven Sea Clan	Summon Dwarves	R2	1/1	Tap: At the end of combat, the Sea Clan deals two points of damage to target attacking or blocking creature. Use this ability only if that creature's controller controls at least one island.
Dwarven Soldier	Summon Dwarf	R1	2/1	If Dwarven Soldier blocks or is blocked by Orcs, it gets +0/+2 until end of turn.
Dwarven Trader	Summon Dwarf	R	1/1	
Dwarven Warriors	Summon Dwarves	R2	1/1	Tap to make a creature with a power of 2 or less unblockable until end of turn.
Earth Elemental	Summon Elemental	RR3	4/5	

Card	Type	Cost	P/T	Description
Earthlink	Enchantment	BRG3	--	During your upkeep pay 2 or bury. Whenever a creature is put into the graveyard from play its controller must sacrifice a land if possible.
Earthlore	Enchant Land	G	--	0: Tap enchanted land to give target blocking creature +1/+2 until end of turn.
Earthquake	Sorcery	RX	--	Does X damage to all players and all non-flying creatures.
Ebon Praetor	Summon Avatar	BB4	5/5	Trample. First strike. During your upkeep, put a -2/-2 counter on Ebon Praetor. You may sacrifice 1 creature to remove a -2/-2 counter from Praetor. If the creature sacrificed was a Thrull, put a +1/+0 counter on Ebon Praetor.
Ebon Stronghold	Land	--	--	Comes into play tapped. Tap to add B to your mana pool. Tap and sacrifice to add BB to your mana pool.
Ebony Horse	Artifact	3	--	Tap+(2) Attacking creature escapes after defense is chosen.
Ebony Rhino	Artifact Creature	7	4/5	Trample.
El-Hajjaj	Summon El-Hajjaj	BB1	1/1	Gain 1 life for each damage El-Hajjaj does to a target.
Elder Druid	Summon Cleric	G3	2/2	Tap+(G3): Elder Druid taps or untaps target artifact, creature, or land.
Elder Land Wurm	Summon Wurm	WWW4	5/5	Cannot attack until it has blocked at least once.
Elemental Augury	Enchantment	UBR	--	3: Look at top 3 cards of target player's library and replace in any order.
Elkin Bottle	Artifact	3	--	Tap+(3) Turn the top card of your library face up in front of you and play it as if it were in your hand; you must play the card by end of turn or discard.
Elven Fortress	Enchantment	G1	--	G1: Target blocking creature gets +0/+1 until end of turn.
Elven Lyre	Artifact	2	--	Tap+(1) and sacrifice to give target creature +2/+2 until end of turn.
Elven Riders	Summon Riders	GG3	3/3	Only blockable by walls and flying creatures.
Elvish Archers	Summon Elves	G1	2/1	First strike.

Card	Type	Cost	P/T	Description
Elvish Farmer	Summon Elf	G1	0/2	During your upkeep put a spore counter on Elvish Farmer. 0: Remove 3 spore counters from Elvish Farmer to put a Saporling token into play. Threat this token as a 1/1 green creature. 0: Sacrifice a Saporling to gain 2 life.
Elvish Healer	Summon Cleric	W2	1/2	Tap to prevent 1 point of damage to any non-green creature or up to 2 points of damage to any green creature in play.
Elvish Hunter	Summon Elf	G1	1/1	Tap+(G1) Keep opponent's creature tapped next turn.
Elvish Scout	Summon Elf	G	1/1	Tap+(G) Untap a target attacking creature you control. That creature neither deals nor receives damage during combat this turn.
Emerald Dragonfly	Summon Dragonfly	G1	1/1	Flying. GG: First strike until end of turn.
Enchantment Alteration	Instant	U	--	Move 1 creature or land enchantment to another creature or land without changing its controller.
Enduring Renewal	Enchantment	WW2	--	Play with the cards in your hand face up. If you draw a creature from your library, discard it. Whenever a creature is removed from player to the graveyard the creature returns to your hand.
Energy Flux	Enchantment	U2	--	Each player must pay 2 for each artifact they control or that artifact is destroyed.
Energy Storm	Enchantment	W1	--	Cumulative upkeep: 1. Damage dealt by instants, interrupts, and sorceries is reduced to 0 as long as Energy Storm remains in play.
Energy Tap	Sorcery	U	--	Taps a creature for colorless mana equal to its casting cost.
Enervate	Instant	U1	--	Tap target artifact, creature, or land in play. Draw a card from the library during the beginning of the next turn's upkeep phase.
Erg Raiders	Summon Raiders	B1	2/3	If do not attack do 2 damage to controller.
Ernham Djinn	Summon Djinn	G3	4/5	Each upkeep, gives one of opponent's creatures forestwalk until next upkeep.
Eron the Relentless	Summon Legend	RR3	5/2	Can attack on the turn it comes into play. RRR: Regenerate.

Card	Type	Cost	P/T	Description
Erosion	Enchant Land	UUU	--	During your opponent's upkeep, he must pay 1 mana or 1 life or else target land is destroyed. Damage from this may not be prevented or redirected.
Errant Minion	Enchant Creature	U2	--	During target creature's controller's upkeep, Errant Minion deals 2 damage to them. They may pay 1 mana for each damage done in this way they wish to prevent.
Errantry	Enchant Creature	R1	--	Target creature gets +3/+0. If it attacks, no other creatures may attack that turn.
Essence Filter	Sorcer	GG1	--	Destroy all enchantments or all non-white enchantments.
Essence Flare	Enchant Creature	U	--	Target creature gets +2/+0. During each of its controller's upkeeps put a -0/-1 counter on creature which remains even if this card is removed.
Essence Vortex	Instant	UB1	--	Bury target creature. That creature's controller may counter by paying the creature's toughness in life.
Eternal Warrior	Enchant Creature	R	--	Target creature does not tap when attacking.
Evaporate	Sorcery	R2		Deals one point of damage to blue and white creaures.
Evil Presence	Enchant Land	B	--	Target land becomes a swamp.
Eye for an Eye	Instant	WW	--	Does damage to opponent equal to the amount done to you by one source.
Faerie Noble	Summon Noble	G2	1/2	Flying. All Faeries you control gain +0/+1. Tap: All Faeries you control get +1/+0 until the end of the turn.
Fallen, The	Summon Fallen	BBB1	2/3	During its controller's upkeep The Fallen does 1 damage to each opponent it has previously damaged.
Fallen Angel	Summon Angel	BB3	3/3	Flying. Sacrifice a creature for +2/+1 until end of turn.
Fanatical Fever	Instant	GG2	--	Target creature gets +3/+0 and trample until end of turn.
Farrel's Mantle	Enchant Creature	W2	--	If target creature attacks and is not blocked, it may deal X+2 damage to any other creature where X is the power of the creature it enchants. If it does so it does not damage opponent this turn.

Card	Type	Cost	P/T	Description
Farrel's Zealot	Summon Townsfolk	WW1	2/2	If Farrel's Zealot attacks and is not blocked, controller may choose to have it deal 3 damage to a target creature. If you do so it deals no damage to opponent this turn.
Farrelite Priest	Summon Cleric	WW1	1/3	1: Add W to your mana pool. If more than 3 is spent in this way then destroy Priest at end of turn.
Fear	Enchant Creature	BB	--	Target may only be blocked by black or artifact creatures.
Feast of the Unicorn	Enchant Creature	B3	--	Target creature gains +4/+0.
Feedback	Enchant Enchantment	U2	--	Feedback does 1 damage to target's controller during his or her upkeep.
Feldon's Cane	Artifact	1	--	Tap to reshuffle your graveyard into your library. Remove Cane from the game.
Fellwar Stone	Artifact	2	--	Tap to add 1 mana to your pool of any color that an opponent's land can generate. This ability is played as an interrupt.
Feral Thallid	Summon Fungus	GGG3	6/3	During your upkeep, put a spore counter on Feral Thallid. 0: Remove 3 spore counters from Feral Thallid to regenerate it.
Feroz's Ban	Artifact	6	--	Summon spells cost 2 extra.
Fiery Justice	Sorcery	WRG	--	Deals 5 damage divided among any number of targets. Target opponent gains 5 life.
Fire Covenant	Instant	BR1	--	Deals X damage, divided in any way to any number of creatures, where X is the amount of life you pay. Damage cannot be prevented.
Fire Drake	Summon Drake	RR1	1/2	Flying. R: +1/+0 until end of turn. No more than R may be spent in this way during one turn.
Fire Elemental	Summon Elemental	RR3	5/4	
Fireball	Sorcery	RX	--	X damage to target each extra target costs one extra mana, split damage evenly, rounded down.
Firebreathing	Enchant Creature	R	--	R: +1/+0 until end of turn.

Card	Type	Cost	P/T	Description
Fishliver Oil	Enchant Creature	U1	--	Give target creatures islandwalk.
Fissure	Instant	RR3	--	Bury any land or creature in play.
Flame Spirit	Summon Spirit	R4	2/3	R: +1/+0 until end of turn.
Flare	Instant	R2	--	Deals 1 damage to target creature or player. Draw a card at the beginning of the next turn's upkeep.
Flash Flood	Instant	U	--	Destroys red permanent or sends mountain in play back to its owner's hand.
Flashfires	Sorcery	R3	--	Destroys all plains in play.
Flight	Enchant Creature	U	--	Target creature gains flying.
Flood	Enchantment	U	--	UU: Target non-flying creature may not attack this turn.
Flooded Woodlands	Enchantment	UB2	--	No green creature can attack unless its controller sacrifices a land.
Flow of Maggots	Summon Insects	B2	2/2	Cumulative upkeep: 1. Flow of Maggots cannot be blocked by any non-wall creatures.
Flying Carpet	Artifact	4	--	Tap+(2) Gives flying to target creature until end of turn. Destroyed if target is destroyed while using it.
Fog	Instant	G	--	Creatures deal and take no damage during combat.
Folk of An-Havva	Summon Folk of An-Havva	G	1/1	If assigned as a blocker, Folk of An-Havva gets +2/+0 until the end of the turn.
Folk of the Pines	Summon Dryads	G4	2/5	G1: +1/+0 until end of turn.
Forbidden Lore	Enchant Land	G2	--	0: Tap enchanted land to give target creature +2/+1 until end of turn.
Force of Nature	Summon Force	GGG G2	8/8	Trample. Controller must pay GGGG during upkeep or Force of Nature does 8 damage to him or her.
Force Void	Interrupt	U2	--	Counters target spell unless the spell's caster pays 1. Draw a card from the library at the beginning of next turn's upkeep phase.
Forest	Land ·	--	--	Tap to add G to your mana pool.

Card	Type	Cost	P/T	Description
Forget	Sorcery	UU	--	Target player chooses and discards two cards from his or her hand. If that player has less than two cards then hand is discarded. Player then draws as many cards as were discarded.
Forgotten Lore	Sorcery	G	--	Opponent chooses a card from your graveyard; you can make him pick another for G, repeating as many times as you like. Place this card in your hand.
Formation	Instant	W1	--	Target creature gains banding until end of turn. Draw a card from the library at the beginning of the next turn's upkeep phase.
Fortified Area	Enchantment	WW1	--	All your walls gain +1/+0 and banding.
Foul Familiar	Summon Spirit	B2	3/1	Cannot block. B: Pay 1 life to return to hand. Damage cannot be prevented.
Fountain of Youth	Artifact	0	--	Tap+(2) Gain 1 life.
Foxfire	Instant	G2	--	Untap target attacking creature. It neither deals nor receives damage this turn. Draw a card at the beginning of the next turn's upkeep.
Freyalise Supplicant	Summon Cleric	G1	1/1	Tap and sacrifice a red or white creature to deal half the creature's power, rounded down, to any target.
Freyalise's Charm	Enchantment	GG	--	GG: Draw a card when opponent successfully casts a black spell. GG: Return Charm to your hand.
Freyalise's Winds	Enchantment	GG2	--	Whenever a permanent is tapped, it gets a wind counter. Does not untap if it has a wind counter on it, but removes counter instead.
Frozen Shade	Summon Shade	B2	0/1	B: +1/+1
Fumarole	Sorcery	BR3	--	Pay 3 life to destroy target creature and target land. Damage cannot be prevented.
Funeral March	Enchant Creature	BB1	--	When target creature leaves play its controller must sacrifice a creature he or she controls if any are in play.
Fungal Bloom	Enchantment	GG	--	GG: Put a spore counter on a target fungus.
Fungusaur	Summon Fungusaur	G3	2/2	Gets a +1/+1 token when damaged and not killed.

Card	Type	Cost	P/T	Description
Fylgja	Enchant Creature	W	--	When Fylgja comes into play put 4 healing counters on it. 0: Remove a counter to prevent 1 damage to creature it enchants. W2: Put a healing counter on Flygja.
Fyndhorn Bow	Artifact	2	--	Tap+(3) Target creature gains first strike ability until the end of turn.
Fyndhorn Brownie	Summon Brownie	G2	1/1	Tap+(G2): Untap target creature.
Fyndhorn Elder	Summon Elf	G2	1/1	Tap to add GG to your mana pool.
Fyndhorn Elves	Summon Elves	G	1/1	Tap to add G to your mana pool.
Fyndhorn Pollen	Enchantment	G2	--	Cumulative upkeep: 1. All creatures get -1/-0. G1: All creatures get -1/-0 until end of turn.
Gabriel Angelfire	Summon Legend	GG WW3	4/4	Each upkeep can get flying, first strike, trample, or rampage: 3 until beginning of next upkeep.
Gaea's Liege	Summon Gaea's Liege	GGG3	*/*	Where * is number of forests opponent has in play when attacking and is number of forests controller has at all other times. Tap to turn any land in play into a forest.
Game of Chaos	Sorcery	RRR	--	Flip a coin. Your favor: gain 1 life and opponent loses 1 life. Opponent's favor: lose 1 life and opponent gains 1 life. Damage cannot be prevented. Stakes double each round.
Gangrenous Zombies	Summon Zombies	BB1	2/2	Tap and sacrifice to deal 1 damage to each creature and player or 2 damage if you control any snow-covered swamps.
Gaseous Form	Enchant Creature	U2	--	Target creature does not deal or take damage in combat.
Gauntlets of Chaos	Artifact Creature	5	--	5: Sacrifice to swap permanent you control with opponent's land or artifact until end of game. Any enchantments on these cards are destroyed.
Gaze of Pain	Sorcery	B1	--	Unblocked attacking creatures may choose not to attack to deal damage to target creature.

Card	Type	Cost	P/T	Description
General Jarkeld	Summon Legend	W3	1/2	Tap to switch the blockers of two target attacking creatures. Must remain legal blocks. Use Ganeral Jarkels's ability only during combat after defense has been chosen and before damage is dealt.
Ghazban Ogre	Summon Ogre	G	2/2	During controller's upkeep, player with highest life total gains control of Ogre.
Ghost Hounds	Summon Hounds	B1	1/1	Attacking does not cause the Hounds to tap. They gain first strike when blocking or blocked by white creatures.
Ghost Ship	Summon Ship	UU2	2/4	Flying. UUU: Regenerates.
Ghostly Flame	Enchantment	BR	--	Both black and red permanents in play and spells cast are considered colorless sources of damage.
Giant Albatross	Summon Albatross	U1	1/1	Flying. B1: Bury creatures that blocked and damaged Albatross when it is put in play from the graveyard. Creature's controller may spend two life to prevent.
Giant Growth	Instant	G	--	Target creature gains +3/+3 until end of turn.
Giant Oyster	Summon Oyster	UU2	0/3	You can choose not to untap Oyster. Tap: Target creature does not untap during controller's untap phase as long as Oyster is tapped. During your upkeep place a -1/-1 counter on that creature. If Oyster is untapped or removed, remove all counters from that creature.
Giant Slug	Summon Slug	B1	1/1	5: Gains basic landwalk ability at the start of your next upkeep until end of that turn.
Giant Spider	Summon Spider	G3	2/4	Is not flying but can block flying creatures.
Giant Strength	Enchant Creature	RR	--	Target creature gains +2/+2.
Giant Tortoise	Summon Tortoise	U1	1/1	Gains +0/+3 if untapped.
Giant Trap Door Spider	Summon Spider	GR1	2/3	Tap+(GR1): Remove target creature without flying that is attacking you from the game, along with Spider.
Glacial Chasm	Land	--	--	Cumulative upkeep of 2 life. Sacrifice a land when it comes into play. Your creatures cannot attack and all damage dealt to you is reduced to 0.

Card	Type	Cost	P/T	Description
Glacial Crevasses	Enchantment	R2	--	0: Sacrifice a snow-covered mountain in play. No creatures may deal damage in combat this turn.
Glacial Wall	Summon Wall	U2	0/7	Wall.
Glaciers	Enchantment	WU2	--	Controller must pay WU during upkeep or destroy Glaciers. Mountains become plains while it remains in play.
Glasses of Urza	Artifact	1	--	Tap to look at opponent's hand.
Gloom	Enchantment	B2	--	White spells and white enchantments cost 3 more.
Goblin Artisans	Summon Goblins	R	1/1	Tap when you cast an artifact and then flip a coin with opponent calling heads or tails. If in opponent's favor, artifact is countered; if in your favor draw a card.
Goblin Balloon Brigade	Summon Goblins	R	1/1	R: Flying until end of turn.
Goblin Chirurgeon	Summon Goblin	R	0/2	0: Sacrifice a Goblin to regenerate target creature.
Goblin Digging Team	Summon Goblins	R	1/1	Sacrifice this card to destroy a wall.
Goblin Flotilla	Summon Goblins	R2	2/2	Islandwalk. At the beginning of the attack, pay R or any creatures blocking or blocked by Goblin Flotilla gain first strike until end of turn.
Goblin Grenade	Sorcery	R	--	Sacrifice a Goblin to do 5 damage to 1 target.
Goblin King	Summon Goblin King	RR1	2/2	All Goblins get +1/+1 and mountainwalk.
Goblin Kites	Enchantment	R1	--	R: A target creature you control which cannot have a toughness greater than 2 gains flying until end of turn. Other effects may be used later to increase the creature's toughness. At end of turn flip a coin, opponent calls heads or tails. If the flip is in opponent's favor bury the creature.
Goblin Lyre	Artifact	3	--	0: Sacrifice Goblin Lyre. Flip a coin. Opponent wins: does X damage to you where X is number of creatures opponent controls. You win: Does X damage to opponent where X is the number of creatures you control.

Card	Type	Cost	P/T	Description
Goblin Mutant	Summon Goblin	RR2	5/3	Trample. Cannot attack if defender has an untapped creature with a power greater than 2.
Goblin Rock Sled	Summon Rock Sled	R1	3/1	Trample. May not attack unless opponent controls at least 1 mountain. Does not untap as normal during untap phase if it attacked during your last turn.
Goblin Sappers	Summon Goblins	R1	1/1	Tap+(RR): Target creature you control cannot be blocked this turn. At the end of turn destroy target and Sappers. Tap+(RRRR): Target creature you control cannot be blocked this turn. Destroy target creature after combat.
Goblin Shrine	Enchant Land	RR1	--	If target land is a basic mountain all goblins in play gain +1/+0. Does 1 damage to all goblins if it leaves play.
Goblin Ski Patrol	Summon Goblins	R1	1/1	R1: Flying and +2/+0. Bury at end of turn. Can only be used if you control snow-covered mountain and can only be used once.
Goblin Snowman	Summon Goblins	R3	1/1	When blocking neither deals nor receives damage. Tap to deal 1 damage to target creature it blocks.
Goblin War Drums	Enchantment	R2	--	Each attacking creature you control that opponent chooses to block may not be blocked with fewer than 2 creatures.
Goblin Warrens	Enchantment	R2	--	R2: Sacrifice 2 Goblins to put 3 goblin tokens into play, treat these tokens as 1/1 red creatures.
Goblins of the Flarg	Summon Goblins	R	1/1	Mountainwalk. This card is buried if controller also controls any Dwarves.
Gorilla Pack	Summon Gorilla Pack	G2	3/3	Cannot attack if opponent has no forests. Bury if you have no forests.
Grandmother Sengir	Summon Legend	B4	3/3	B1 and tap: Target creature gets -1/-1 until the end of the turn.
Grapeshot Catapult	Artifact Creature	4	2/3	Tap to do 1 damage to any flying creature.
Gravebind	Instant	B	--	Target creature is unable to regenerate this turn. During the next upkeep phase draw a card from your library.
Gray Ogre	Summon Ogre	R2	2/2	

Card	Type	Cost	P/T	Description
Greater Werewolf	Summon Lycanthrope	B4	2/4	At the end of combat place a -0/-2 counter on all creatures blocking or blocked by Greater Werewolf.
Greed	Enchantment	B3	--	B: Draw a card and lose 2 life. Loss of life cannot be prevented or redirected.
Green Mana Battery	Artifact	4	--	Tap+(2) Add a token to Battery. Tap to add G to your mana pool. Can also convert tokens to G.
Green Scarab	Enchant Creature	W	--	Target creature gets +2/+2 as long as opponent controls any green cards and cannot be blocked by green creatures.
Green Ward	Enchant Creature	W	--	Target creature gains protection from green.
Grizzled Wolverine	Summon Wolverine	RR1	2/2	R: +2/+0 until end of turn. Can only be used once and only when blocked.
Grizzly Bears	Summon Bears	G1	2/2	
Hallowed Ground	Enchantment	W1	--	WW: Return target land you control to owner's hand.
Halls of Mist	Land	--	--	Cumulative upkeep of 1. No creatures can attack if they attacked during their controller's last turn.
Hand of Justice	Summon Avatar	W5	2/6	Tap 3 white creatures you control to destroy target creature.
Hasran Ogress	Summon Ogre	BB	3/2	Pay 2 when it attacks or take 3 damage.
Havenwood Battleground	Land	--	--	Comes into play tapped. Tap to add G to your mana pool. Tap and sacrifice to add GG to your mana pool.
Hazduhr the Abbot	Summon Legend	WW3	2/5	X, Tap: Redirect X damage dealt to a white creature back to Hazduhr the Abbot.
Headstone	Instant	B1	--	Draw a card at the during the next turn's upkeep. Remove target card in any graveyard from the game.
Heal	Instant	W	--	Prevent 1 damage to any creature or player. Draw a card from the library at the beginning of the next turn's upkeep phase.
Healing Salve	Instant	W	--	Gain 3 life or prevent 3 damage to one target.

Card	Type	Cost	P/T	Description
Heart Wolf	Summon Wolf	R3	2/2	First strike. Tap: Target Dwarf gets first strike and +2/+0 until end of turn. If Dwarf leaves play bury Heart Wolf. This ability must be used before attack and defense is chosen.
Hecatomb	Enchantment	BB1	--	When Hecatomb enters play its caster must sacrafice 4 creatures. 0: Swamps you control may be tapped to have Hecatomb cause 1 point of damage to target creature or player.
Hell's Caretaker	Summon Hell's Caretaker	B3	1/1	Tap and sacrifice a creature during upkeep to bring a creature from your graveyard directly into play.
Helm of Chatzuk	Artifact	1	--	Tap+(1) Gives target creature banding until end of turn.
Hematite Talisman	Artifact	2	--	3: Untap target permanent in play. Use this ability only when a red spell is cast successfully and only once for each red spell cast.
Heroism	Enchantment	W2	--	0: Sacrifice a white creature to have all attacking red creatures deal no damage. Attacking player may spend 2 R to have an attacking creature deal damage as normal.
High Tide	Instant	U	--	Until end of turn all Islands generate an additional U when tapped for mana.
Hill Giant	Summon Giant	R3	3/3	
Hipparion	Summon Hipparion	W1	1/3	Must pay 1 to block a creature with power of 3 or greater.
Hive, The	Artifact	5	--	Tap+(5) Make a 1/1 flying wasp counter.
Hoar Shade	Summon Shade	B3	1/2	B: +1/+1 until end of turn.
Hollow Trees	Land	--	--	Comes into play tapped. May leave tapped to add 1 storage counter. Tap and remove X storage counters to add X G to your mana pool.
Holy Armor	Enchant Creature	W	--	Target creature gains +0/+2 and W: +0/+1 until end of turn.
Holy Strength	Enchant Creature	W	--	Target creature gains +1/+2.

Card	Type	Cost	P/T	Description
Homarid	Summon Homarid	U2	2/2	Put a token on Homarid when it is brought into play and during your up-keep. If there is 1 counter on Homarid, it gets -1/-1. If there are 3 counters on Homarid it gets +1/+1. If there are 4 counters on Homarid, remove them all.
Homarid Shaman	Summon Homarid	UU2	2/1	U: Tap a green creature.
Homarid Spawning Bed	Enchantment	UU	--	UU1: Sacrifice a blue creature to put X Camarid tokens in play, where X is the casting cost of the creature. Treat these tokens as 1/1 blue creatures.
Homarid Warrior	Summon Homarid	U4	3/3	U: Warrior may not be the target of spells or fast effects until the end of turn. Does not untap as normal during its controller's next untap phase. If Homarid Warrior is not tapped, tap it.
Horn of Deafening	Artifact	4	--	Tap+(2) Makes creature deal no damage this turn.
Hot Springs	Enchant Land	G1	--	0: Tap enchanted land to prevent 1 damage to a target.
Howl from Beyond	Instant	BX	--	Target creature gains +X/+0 until end of turn.
Howling Mine	Artifact	2	--	Each player must draw an additional card during his draw phase.
Hungry Mist	Summon Mist	GG2	6/2	Pay GG during upkeep or bury Hungry Mist.
Hurkyl's Recall	Instant	U1	--	All of target player's artifacts are returned to his or her hand.
Hurloon Minotaur	Summon Minotaur	RR1	2/3	
Hurr Jackal	Summon Jackal	R	1/1	Tap to prevent target creature from regenerating this turn.
Hurricane	Sorcery	GX	--	Does X damage to all players and all flying creatures.
Hyalopterous Lemure	Summon Lemure	B4	4/3	0: Flying and -0/-1 until end of turn.
Hydroblast	Interrupt	U	--	Counter target spell or destroy target permanent in play if red.
Hymn of Rebirth	Sorcery	GW3	--	Take a creature from a graveyard and put it into play as though it were just summoned.

Card	Type	Cost	P/T	Description
Hymn to Tourach	Sorcery	BB	--	Target player discards 2 cards from his hand. If he does not have 2 cards, entire hand is discarded.
Hypnotic Specter	Summon Specter	BB1	2/2	Flying. If Specter damages opponent, he or she must discard one card at random.
Icatian Infantry	Summon Soldiers	W	1/1	1: Gains banding until end of turn. 1: Gains first strike until end of turn.
Icatian Javelineers	Summon Soldiers	W	1/1	When brought into play put a javelin counter on it. Tap and remove the counter to have Icatian Javelineers deal 1 point of damage to any target.
Icatian Lieutenant	Summon Soldier	WW	1/2	W1: Target soldier gets +1/+0 until end of turn.
Icatian Moneychanger	Summon Townsfolk	W	0/2	Does 3 damage when summoned. Put 3 counters on Moneychanger at that time. During your upkeep, put a counter on Moneychanger. 0: During your upkeep, sacrifice it to gain 1 life for each counter.
Icatian Phalanx	Summon Soldiers	W4	2/4	Banding.
Icatian Priest	Summon Cleric	W	1/1	WW1: Gives target creature +1/+1 until end of turn.
Icatian Scout	Summon Soldier	W	1/1	Tap+(1) Target creature gets +1/+1 until end of turn.
Icatian Skirmishers	Summon Soldiers	W3	1/1	Bands. First strike. All creatures that band with Icatian Skirmishers gain first strike until end of turn.
Icatian Store	Land	--	--	Comes into play tapped. May leave tapped to add 1 storage counter. Tap and remove X storage counters to add X W to your mana pool.
Icatian Town	Sorcery	W5	--	Put 4 citizen tokens in play, treat these as 1/1 white creatures.
Ice Cauldron	Artifact	4	--	Tap+(X) If there are no counters on Ice Cauldron, place a spell card face up on it. Put a charge counters on Cauldron of amount of mana for activation cost. You may play that card as though it were in your hand. Tap to remove the charge counter to add mana of the type and amount used to pay activation cost to your pool. This mana may only be used to cast spell on the Ice Cauldron.

Card	Type	Cost	P/T	Description
Ice Floe	Land	--	--	You may choose not to untap Ice Floe during your untap phase. Tap to tap target creature without flying ability that attacks you. As long as Ice Floe remains tapped so does the creature it tapped.
Iceberg	Enchantment	UUX	--	When comes into play put X ice counters on it. 3: Add an ice counter. 0: Remove an ice counter to add 1 to your mana pool. Use as an interrupt.
Icequake	Sorcery	BB1	--	Destroys target land and does 1 damage to controller if target land is snow-covered.
Icy Manipulator	Artifact	4	--	Tap+(1) Tap any creature, land, or artifact in play. No effects are generated from this card.
Icy Prison	Enchantment	UU	--	When Icy Prison comes into play, remove target creature from the game. When it leaves play, return that creature to play under its owner's control as if it were just summoned. During your upkeep, destroy Icy Prison. Any player may pay 3 to prevent this.
Ihsan's Shade	Summon Legend	BBB3	5/5	Protection from white.
Illusionary Forces	Summon Illusion	U3	4/4	Cumulative upkeep: U. Flying.
Illusionary Presence	Summon Illusion	UU1	2/2	Cumulative upkeep: U. During your upkeep gains a landwalk ability of your choice.
Illusionary Terrain	Enchantment	UU	--	Cumulative upkeep: 2. All basic lands of one type become lands of a different type of your choice as long an Illusionary Terrain remains in play.
Illusionary Wall	Summon Wall	U4	7/4	Cumulative upkeep: U. Flying, first strike.
Illusions of Grandeur	Enchantment	U3	--	Cumulative upkeep: 2. When comes into play gain 20 life. When leaves play lose 20 life. Loss of life cannot be prevented.
Immolation	Enchant Creature	R	--	Target creature gains +2/-2.
Implements of Sacrifice	Artifact	2	--	Tap+(1) Sacrifice to add 2 mana of any color to your pool. Play this ability as an interrupt.

Card	Type	Cost	P/T	Description
Imposing Visage	Enchant Creature	R	--	Target creature can only be blocked by two or more creatures.
Incinerate	Instant	R1	--	Deals 3 damage to target creature or player. Target cannot regenerate.
Indestructible Aura	Instant	W	--	Creature takes no damage for the rest of turn.
Infernal Darkness	Enchantment	BB2	--	Cumulative upkeep: B and 1 life point. All lands that produce mana now produce B instead of their normal mana type.
Infernal Denzien	Summon Infernal Denzien	B7	5/7	During your upkeep sacrifice 2 swamps or becomes tapped and opponent gains control of one of your creatures. Opponent loses control if Denzien leaves play. Tap to take control of target creature. Lose control if Denzien leaves play.
Inferno	Instant	RR5	--	Does 6 damage to all creatures and players.
Infinite Hourglass	Artifact	4	--	During your upkeep, put a time counter on Hourglass. During any upkeep, a player may pay 3 colorless to remove a time counter from Infinite Hourglass. All creatures gain +1/+0 for each time counter remaining on the Hourglass.
Infuse	Instant	U2	--	Untap target artifact, creature, or land in play. Draw a card from the library during the beginning of the next turn's upkeep phase.
Initiates of the Ebon Hand	Summon Clerics	B	1/1	1: Add B to your mana pool. If more than 3 is spent in this fashion, Initiates is destroyed at end of turn.
Instill Energy	Enchant Creature	G	--	Target creature may untap once during your turn in addition to your untap phase. May attack on the turn it is brought into play.
Irini Sengir	Summon Legend	BB2	2/2	White and green enchantments now cost an additional 2.
Iron Star	Artifact	1	--	1: Gain 1 life whenever a red spell is cast.

Card	Type	Cost	P/T	Description
Ironclaw Curse	Enchnat Creature	R	--	Target creature gains -0/-1. That creature can no longer be assigned to block any creature with a power greater than or equal to its toughness.
Ironclaw Orcs	Summon Orcs	R1	2/2	Cannot be assigned to block creatures of power greater than 1.
Ironroot Treefolk	Summon Treefolk	G4	3/5	
Ishan's Shade	Summon Legend	BBB3	5/5	Protection from white.
Island	Land	--	--	Tap to add U to your mana pool.
Island Fish Jasconius	Summon Island Fish	UUU4	6/8	Does not untap as normal. Pay UUU during your upkeep to untap Island Fish. Cannot attack if your opponent does not have islands. Destroyed if at any time you don't have islands in play.
Island Sanctuary	Enchantment	W1	--	You may choose not to draw a card to limit attacks on you to creatures that have flying or islandwalk.
Ivory Cup	Artifact	1	--	1: Gain 1 life whenever a white spell is cast.
Ivory Guardians	Summon Guardians	WW4	3/3	Protection from red. Gets +1/+1 if opponent has red cards in play.
Ivory Tower	Artifact	1	--	During your upkeep you gain 1 life for each card over 4 in your hand.
Jade Monolith	Artifact	4	--	1: Transfer damage to self from creature.
Jalum Tome	Artifact	3	--	Tap+(2) Draw a card and then discard a card of your choice.
Jandor's Saddlebags	Artifact	2	--	Tap+(3) Untap a creature.
Jayemdae Tome	Artifact	4	--	Tap+(4) Draw a card.
Jester's Cap	Artifact	4	--	Tap+(2) Sacrifice to search target player's library and remove 3 cards from the game. Reshuffle after.
Jester's Mask	Artifact	5	--	Comes into play tapped. Tap+(1) Sacrifice to look at opponent's hand and library. Replace hand with same number of cards. Reshuffle.
Jeweled Amulet	Artifact	0	--	Tap+(1) Put charge counter on Amulet. Tap to remove charge counter to add 1 mana of type used to place counter to pool. Play as an interrupt.

Card	Type	Cost	P/T	Description
Jeweled Bird	Artifact	1	--	Tap to exchange for your ante and draw a new card. Bury old ante.
Jinx	Instant	U1	--	Target land becomes a basic land type of your choice until end of turn. Draw a card at the beginning of the next upkeep.
Johan	Summon Legend	GRW3	5/4	If Johan does not attack and is not tapped then none of your creatures tap when attacking.
Johtull Wurm	Summon Wurm	G5	6/6	For each creature more than one that blocks it, it gets -2/-1 until end of turn.
Jokulhaups	Sorcery	RR4	--	Bury all artifacts, creatures, and lands.
Joven	Summon Legend	RR3	3/3	RRR, tap: Destroy target non-creature artifact.
Joven's Ferrets	Summon Ferrets	G	1/1	If declared as an attacker Joven's Ferrets gain +0/+2. If blocked tap the creature that blocked the Ferrets at the end of combat. That creature will not untap during its controller's next untap phase.
Joven's Tools	Artifact	6	--	4 and tap: Target creature cannot be blocked except by walls until end of the turn.
Jovial Evil	Sorcery	B2	--	Opponent takes 2 damage for each white creature controlled.
Jump	Instant	U	--	Target creature gains flight until end of turn.
Juniper Order Druid	Summon Cleric	G2	1/1	Tap to untap target land. Use this ability as an interrupt.
Junun Efreet	Summon Efreet	BB1	3/3	Flying. Pay BB during your upkeep or Junan is destroyed.
Justice	Enchantment	WW2	--	During your upkeep pay WW or destroy it. When a red spell or creature does damage, Justice does equal damage to its controller. Not affected by subsequent reduction of damage.
Juxtapose	Sorcery	U3	--	You and opponent trade control of both your highest casting cost creature and your highest casting cost artifact.
Karma	Enchantment	WW2	--	Each player takes 1 damage during his upkeep for each swamp he controls.

Card	Type	Cost	P/T	Description
Karplusan Forest	Land	--	--	Tap to add 1 colorless to your mana pool or tap to add R to your mana pool and suffer 1 damage or tap to add G to your mana pool and suffer 1 damage.
Karplusan Giant	Summon Giant	R6	3/3	0: Tap a snow-covered land you control to give +1/+1 until end of turn.
Karplusan Yeti	Summon Yeti	RR3	3/3	Tap to deal damage to target creatures equal to its power. Takes damage equal to target's power.
Keepers of the Faith	Summon Keepers	WW1	2/3	
Kei Takahashi	Summon Legend	GW2	2/2	Tap to prevent up to 2 damage to a creature.
Keldon Warlord	Summon Lord	RR2	*/*	Where * is the number of creatures controller has in play.
Kelsinko Ranger	Summon Ranger	W	1/1	W1: Target green creature gains first strike ability until end of turn.
Killer Bees	Summon Bees	GG1	0/1	Flying. G: +1/+1 until end of turn.
Kismet	Enchantment	W3	--	All of opponent's lands, creatures, and artifacts come into play tapped.
Kjeldoran Dead	Summon Dead	B	3/1	When it comes into play, sacrifice a creature. B: Regenerate.
Kjeldoran Elite Guard	Summon Soldier	W3	2/2	Tap to give target creature +2/+2 until end of turn. If target leaves play this turn, bury this card too. Use only when attack or defense is announced.
Kjeldoran Frostbeast	Summon Frostbeast	WG3	2/4	At end of combat, destroy all creatures blocking/blocked by Frostbeast.
Kjeldoran Guard	Summon Soldier	W1	1/1	Tap to give target creature +1/+1 until end of turn. If target leaves play this turn, bury this card, too. Use only when attack or defense is announced and opponent has no snow-covered lands.
Kjeldoran Knight	Summon Knight	WW	1/1	Banding. W1: +1/+0 until end of turn. WW: +0/+2 until end of turn.
Kjeldoran Phalanx	Summon Soldiers	W5	2/5	Banding.
Kjeldoran Royal Guard	Summon Soldiers	WW3	2/5	Tap to redirect all damage done to you from unblocked creatures to Guard.
Kjeldoran Skycaptain	Summon Soldier	W4	2/2	Banding, flying, first strike.

Card	Type	Cost	P/T	Description
Kjeldoran Skyknight	Summon Soldier	W2	1/1	Banding, flying, first strike.
Kjeldoran Warrior	Summon Hero	W	1/1	Banding.
Knights of Stromgald	Summon Knight	BB	2/1	Protection from white. BB: +1/+0 to end of turn. B: First strike to end of turn.
Kormus Bell	Artifact	4	--	All swamps in play are considered 1/1 creatures.
Koskun Falls	Enchant World	BB2	--	During upkeep tap untapped creature you control or bury Falls. Creature cannot attack unless its controller pays 2 for each attacking creature.
Koskun Keep	Land	--	--	Tap to add one colorless mana to your mana pool. Tap and pay one colorless to add one R to your mana pool. Tap and pay two and add one B or one G to pool.
Krovikan Elementalist	Summon Wizard	BB	1/1	R2: Target creature gets +1/+0 bonus to power until end of turn. UU: Target creature you control gains flying ability until end of turn; bury it at end of turn.
Krovikan Fetish	Enchant Creature	B2	--	Target creature gains a +1/+1 bonus to power and toughess. Draw a card from your library during next upkeep phase.
Krovikan Sorcerer	Summon Wizard	U2	1/1	Tap to choose one card from your hand and draw another. If discarded card was black draw two cards instead, keep one and discard the other.
Krovikan Vampire	Summon Vampire	BB3	3/3	If it damages a creature that dies that turn, creature comes into play under your control. If you lose control of Vampire or it leaves play, bury the creature.
Labyrinth Minotaur	Summon Minotaur	U3	1/4	Creatures do not untap during their controller's next untap phase if blocked by Labyrinth Minotaur.
Land Cap	Land	--	--	Does not untap during controller's untap phase if it has a depletion counter. During upkeep remove 1 counter. Tap to add W or U to your mana pool and add a depletion counter to Land Cap.
Land Leeches	Summon Leeches	GG1	2/2	First strike.

Card	Type	Cost	P/T	Description
Land Tax	Enchantment	W	--	If opponent controls more land than you during your upkeep you may search through your library and withdraw up to three basic lands. Reshuffle your library.
Land's Edge	Enchant World	RR1	--	Any player may discard a card at any time. If discarded card is a land may do 2 damage to any player.
Lapis Lazuli Talisman	Artifact	2	--	3: Untap a target permanent in play. Use only when blue spells are cast and only once for each.
Lava Burst	Sorcery	RX	--	Does X damage to target creature or player. Cannot be prevented or redirected.
Lava Tubes	Land	--	--	Does not untap if it has a depletion counter on it. During upkeep remove 1 depletion counter. Tap to add B to your mana pool and put one depletion counter on Lava Tubes or tap to add R to your mana pool and put one depletion counter on it.
Leaping Lizard	Summon Lizard	GG1	2/3	G1: Flying and -0/-1 until end of turn.
Leeches	Sorcery	WW1	--	Target player loses all poison counters. Leeches deal one damage to that player for each poison counter removed in this fashion.
Legions of Lim-Dul	Summon Zombies	BB1	2/3	Snow-covered swampwalk.
Leshrac's Rite	Enchant Creature	B	--	Target creature gains swampwalk ability.
Leshrac's Sigil	Enchantment	BB	--	BB: When an opponent successfully casts a green spell, you may look at his hand and choose one card that he must discard. BB: Return Leshrac's Sigil from play to its owner's hand.
Leviathan	Summon Leviathan	UUUU5	10/10	Trample. When Leviathan comes into play you must sacrifice 2 islands. In order to attack, you must sacrifice 2 islands. To untap you must sacrifice 2 islands.
Ley Druid	Summon Cleric	G2	1/1	Tap to untap any 1 land in play.

Card	Type	Cost	P/T	Description
Lhurgoyf	Summon Lhurgoyf	GG2	*/1+*	Where * is the number of creatures in all graveyards.
Library of Leng	Artifact	1	--	Skip discard phase. Discard to top of library.
Lifeforce	Enchantment	GG	--	GG: Counters target black spell as it is being cast.
Lifelace	Interrupt	G	--	Changes color of target permanent to green.
Lifetap	Enchantment	UU	--	You gain 1 life whenever opponent taps a forest.
Lightening Blow	Instant	W1	--	Target creature gains first strike capability until end of turn. Draw a card at the next turn's upkeep.
Lightning Bolt	Instant	R	--	Does 3 damage to any target.
Lim-Dul's Cohort	Summon Zombies	BB1	2/3	Creatures blocking/blocked by this creature cannot regenerate this turn.
Lim-Dul's Hex	Enchantment	B1	--	During its controller's upkeep Lim-Dul's Hex inflicts 1 point of damage to each player. This damage can be prevented by playing B or 3. By paying this the damage is prevented to the player and not the opponent.
Living Armor	Artifact	4	--	Tap to sacrifice Living Armor to put +0/+X token on target creature.
Living Artifact	Enchant Artifact	G	--	Put one token on artifact for each life lost. Can convert one token to 1 life during your upkeep.
Living Lands	Enchantment	G3	--	Treat all forests in play as 1/1 creatures.
Llanowar Elves	Summon Elves	G	1/1	Tap to add G to your mana pool.
Lord of Atlantis	Summon Lord	UU	2/2	Gives all Merfolk in play +1/+1.
Lord of the Pit	Summon Demon	BBB4	7/7	Trample. First strike. Sacrifice 1 creature every upkeep or does seven damage to you.
Lost Order of Jarkeld	Summon Knights	WW2	1+*/1+*	Has power and toughness equal to 1+number of creatures opponent controls.
Lost Soul	Summon Lost Soul	BB1	2/1	Swampwalk.
Lure	Enchant Creature	GG1	--	All creatures able to block target creature must do so.

Card	Type	Cost	P/T	Description
Maddening Wind	Enchant Creature	G2	--	Cumulative upkeep: G. Does 2 damage to target's controller during upkeep.
Magical Hack	Interrupt	U	--	Change a land reference on one card.
Magnetic Mountain	Enchantment	RR1	--	Blue creatures cost 4 to untap during upkeep.
Magus of the Unseen	Summon Wizard	U1	1/1	Tap+U1: Untap target artifact in play opponent controls and gain control of it until end of turn. If that artifact is a creature, it can attack and you may use any abilities that require tapping. When you lose control of it, tap it.
Mahamoti Djinn	Summon Djinn	UU4	5/6	Flying.
Malachite Talisman	Artifact	2	--	3: Untap target permanent in play. Use only when green spells are cast and only once for each.
Mammoth Harness	Enchant Creature	G3	--	Target creature loses flying. Any creature blocking or blocked by creature enchanted by Harness gains first strike until the end of the turn.
Mana Clash	Sorcery	R	--	You and target player each flip a coin. Does 1 damage to any player whose coin comes up tails. Repeat until both player's coins come up heads at the same time.
Mana Flare	Enchantment	R2	--	All mana producing lands produce 1 extra mana.
Mana Short	Instant	U2	--	All of opponent's land is tapped and their mana pool is emptied.
Mana Vault	Artifact	1	--	Tap to add 3 to your mana pool. Untap for 4 mana during your upkeep or take 1 damage.
Manabarbs	Enchantment	R3	--	1 damage to anyone who taps a land.
Marhault Elsdragon	Summon Legend	GRR3	4/6	Rampage: 1.
Marjhan	Summon Serpent	UU5	8/8	Marjhan does not untap during your untap phase. Marjhan cannot attack if defending player has no islands. If controller has no islands bury Marjhan. UU: Sacrifice creature to untap Marjhan. UU: -1/-0 until end of turn. Marjhan deals one damage to target attacking creature without flying.

Card	Type	Cost	P/T	Description
Marsh Gas	Instant	B	--	All creatures get -2/-0 until end of turn.
Marsh Viper	Summon Viper	G3	1/2	If Marsh Viper damages opponent, opponent gets 2 poison counters. If opponent ever has 10 or more poison counters, opponent loses game.
Marton Stromgald	Summon Legend	RR2	1/1	If attacking all other attacking creatures gain +*/+* where * is the number of attacking creatures. If blocking all other blockers gain +*/+* where * is the number of blocking creatures.
Meekstone	Artifact	1	--	Creatures with power greater than 2 do not untap as normal.
Melee	Instant	R4	--	Play when you attack, choose how defenders block. Unblocked attackers are untapped and treated as if they didn't attack.
Melting	Enchantment	R3	--	All snow-covered lands become normal lands.
Memory Lapse	Interupt	U1	--	Counter target spell. Put spell back on top of owner's library.
Mercenaries	Summon Mercenaries	W3	3/3	Whenever it damages a player, he or she must pay 3 to prevent.
Merchant Scroll	Scorcery	U1	--	Search your library for a blue instant or interrupt. Reveal that card to all players and put it in your hand. Reshuffle your library.
Merfolk of the Pearl Trident	Summon Merfolk	U	1/1	
Merieke Ri Berit	Summon Legend	WUB	1/1	Does not untap during untap phase. Tap to gain control of target creature. Lose control of creature if you lose control of Merieke Ri Berit. Bury target if it becomes untapped or leaves play.
Merseine	Enchant Creature	UU2	--	Put 3 net counters on Merseine when it is brought into play. Target creature Merseine enchants does not untap as normal during its controller's upkeep as long as Merseine has net counters on it. As a fast effect, target creature's controller may pay the creature's casting cost to remove a counter from Merseine.
Mesa Falcon	Summon Falcon	W1	1/1	1W: +0/+1 until end of turn. Flying.

Card	Type	Cost	P/T	Description
Mesa Pegasus	Summon Pegasus	W1	1/1	Flying. Banding.
Mesmeric Trance	Enchantment	UU1	--	Cumulative upkeep: 1. U: Discard a card from your hand to the graveyard to draw a card.
Metamorphosis	Sorcery	G	--	Sacrifice creature for casting cost plus one of any color mana. Mana may only be used for summoning spells.
Meteor Shower	Sorcery	RXX	--	Deals X+1 damage divided among any number of targets.
Millstone	Artifact	2	--	Tap+(2) Opponent discards 2 cards from top of library.
Mind Bomb	Sorcery	U	--	All players must discard 3 cards from their hand or suffer 1 damage for each card they do not discard.
Mind Ravel	Sorcery	B2	--	Target player discards a card of choice from his hand. Draw a card at the beginning of next turn's upkeep.
Mind Twist	Sorcery	BX	--	Target player must discard X cards. If he does not have X cards, entire hand is discarded.
Mind Warp	Sorcery	B3X	--	Look at target player's hand and force him to discard X cards of your choice.
Mind Whip	Enchant Creature	2BB	--	Target creature's controller suffers 2 points of damage dealt by Mind Whip unless he or she pays 3. If Mind Whip damages creature's controller in this manner, tap that creature.
Mindstab Thrull	Summon Thrull	BB1	2/2	If it attacks and is not blocked you may sacrifice Mindstab to force opponent to discard 3 cards at random from hand. If so it deals no damage during this combat. If player does not have enough cards his entire hand is discarded.
Minion of Leshrac	Summon Demon	BBB4	5/5	Protection from black. During your upkeep sacrifice a creature or deals 5 damage to you and becomes tapped. Cannot be sacrificed to itself. Tap to destroy a creature or land.
Minion of Tevesh Szat	Summon Demon	BBB4	4/4	During your upkeep, pay BB or deals 2 damage to you. Tap to give target creature +3/-2 until end of turn.

Card	Type	Cost	P/T	Description
Mishra's Factory	Land	--	--	Tap to add 1 colorless mana to your pool. (1) Mishra's Factory becomes an assembly worker until end of turn. Tap to add +1/+1 to any assembly worker until end of turn.
Mishra's War Machine	Artifact Creature	7	5/5	During your upkeep you must discard a card from your hand. If you do not you take 3 damage and it becomes tapped.
Mistfolk	Summon Mistfolk	UU	1/2	U: Counter target spell that targets it.
Mole Worms	Summon Worms	B2	1/1	You may choose not to untap Mole Worms during untap. Tap to tap target land. As long as Worms remains tapped, so does land.
Mons's Goblin Raiders	Summon Goblins	R	1/1	
Monsoon	Enchantment	2RG	--	When an island is tapped, controller takes 1 damage at end of turn.
Moor Fiend	Summon Fiend	B3	3/3	Swampwalk.
Morale	Instant	WW1	--	All attacking creatures gain +1/+1 until end of turn.
Mountain	Land	--	--	Tap to add R to your mana pool.
Mountain Goat	Summon Goat	R	1/1	Mountainwalk.
Mountain Titan	Summon Titan	BR2	2/2	RR1: For the rest of the turn, put a +1/+1 counter on Titan whenever you cast a black spell.
Mountain Yeti	Summon Yeti	RR2	3/3	Mountainwalk. Protection from white.
Mudslide	Enchantment	R2	--	Creatures without flying do not untap as normal. Controller may pay 2 during upkeep to untap a creature.
Murk Dwellers	Summon Murk Dwellers	B3	2/2	When attacking, Murk Dwellers gain +2/+0 if not blocked.
Musician	Summon Mage	U2	1/3	Cumulative upkeep: 1. Tap to place a music counter on target creature in play. During that creature's controller's upkeep phase he or she pays 1 mana for each counter or the creature is destroyed.
Mystic Decree	Enchant World	UU2	--	All creatures lose flying and islandwalking ablilities.

Card	Type	Cost	P/T	Description
Mystic Might	Enchant Land	U	--	Cumulative upkeep: U1. When it comes into play choose target land you control. 0: Tap enchanted land to give target creature in play +2/+2 until the end of the turn.
Mystic Remora	Enchantment	U	--	Cumulative upkeep: 1. When opponent successfully casts a non-creature spell, you may draw an extra card. Opponent may counter this effect by paying 4 colorless.
Nacre Talisman	Artifact	2	--	3: Untap target permanent in play. Use only when white spells are cast and only once for each.
Naf's Asp	Summon Asp	G	1/1	If damages opponent, he must pay 1 during his next upkeep or take an additional damage.
Naked Singularity	Artifact	5	--	Cumulative upkeep: 3. Instead of producing their normal mana, plains produce R mana, islands produce G mana, swamps produce W mana, mountains produce U mana, and forests produce B mana.
Narwhal	Summon Narwhal	UU2	2/2	First strike, protection from red.
Nature's Lore	Sorcery	G1	--	Search your library for a forest and put it into play. Does not count as your land for the turn.
Nebuchadnezzar	Summon Legend	BU3	3/3	Tap+(X) Name a card and look at X cards from opponent's hand. If named card is present in revealed cards, it is discarded. Can only be used on your turn.
Necrite	Summon Thrull	BB1	2/2	If Necrite attacks and is not blocked you may sacrifice it to bury target creature controlled by the player it attacked this round. If you do this, Necrite deals no damage in combat this turn.
Necropotence	Enchantment	BBB	--	Once Necropotence is in play you skip your draw phase from that point on. If you discard a card from your hand that card is removed from the game. 0: Pay 1 life and set aside a card from the top of your library and place in your hand at the next discard phase. Damage cannot be redirected or prevented.

Card	Type	Cost	P/T	Description
Nether Shadow	Summon Shadow	B	1/1	If Nether Shadow is in the graveyard and 3 creatures are above it, then it comes into play during your upkeep phase.
Nevinyrral's Disk	Artifact	4	--	Tap+(1) Destroys all creatures, artifacts, and enchantments in play. Comes into play tapped.
Nicol Bolas	Summon Elder Dragon Legend	BBUU RR2	7/7	Flying. If opponent is damaged by Nicol he or she must discard their entire hand. During upkeep pay BUR or this card is buried.
Night Soil	Enchantment	GG	--	1: Remove 2 creatures in any graveyard from play to put a Saporling token into play. Treat this token as a 1/1 green creature.
Nightmare	Summon Nightmare	B5	*/*	Flying. Where * is the number of swamps you have in play.
Norritt	Summon Imp	B3	1/1	Tap to untap target blue creature. Tap to force a non-wall creature to attack. If cannot it is destroyed at end of turn.
Northern Paladin	Summon Paladin	WW2	3/3	Tap+(WW) Destroy any black card in play.
Oasis	Land	--	--	Tap to prevent 1 damage to any creature.
Oath of Lim-Dul	Enchantment	B3	--	For each damage you suffer discard a card from play or from your hand. You may not remove Oath of Lim-Dul in this mannner unless you no longer control any permanents and have no cards in your hand except for the Oath of Lim-Dul. BB: Draw a card.
Obelisk of Undoing	Artifact	1	--	6: Return one of your permanents in play to your hand.
Obsianus Golem	Artifact Creature	6	4/6	
Onulet	Artifact Creature	3	2/2	If Onulet dies you gain 2 life.
Onyx Talisman	Artifact	2	--	3: Untap target permanent in play. Use this ability only when black spells are cast and only once for each black spell cast.
Orcish Artillery	Summon Orcs	RR1	1/3	Tap to do 2 damage to any target. Then does 3 damage to controller.

Card	Type	Cost	P/T	Description
Orcish Cannoneers	Summon Orcs	RR1	1/3	Tap to do 2 damage to any target and 3 damage to you.
Orcish Captain	Summon Orc	R	1/1	1: Choose a target Orc. Flip a coin. If in your favor that Orc gets +2/+0 until end of turn; if in opponent's favor Orc gets -0/-2 until end of turn.
Orcish Conscripts	Summon Orcs	R	2/2	Cannot attack or block unless 2 other creatures are attacking or blocking.
Orcish Farmer	Summon Orc	RR1	2/2	Tap to change target land to a swamp until its controller's next upkeep.
Orcish Healer	Summon Cleric	RR	1/1	Tap+(RR): Target creature cannot regenerate this turn. Tap+(RBB) or Tap+(RGG): Regenerate target black or green creature.
Orcish Librarian	Summon Orc	R1	1/1	Tap+(R): Take the top 8 cards of your library, remove 4 of the 8 at random, and replace remaining 4 in any order on top of library.
Orcish Lumberjack	Summon Orc	R	1/1	Tap and sacrifice a forest to add 3 mana in any combination of red and green to your mana pool. Play as an interrupt.
Orcish Mine	Enchant Land	RR1	--	When comes into play place three counters on it. Each time enchanted land is tapped remove a counter. When no more counters are on Mine, destroy land and deal two points of damage to its controller.
Orcish Oriflamme	Enchantment	RR1	--	All your attacking creatures gain +1/+0.
Orcish Spy	Summon Orc	R	1/1	Tap to look at top 3 cards of target player's library and then return them in the same order.
Orcish Squatters	Summon Orcs	R4	2/3	If attacks and not blocked you gain control of target land. Lose if you lose control of Squatters or if they leave play.
Orcish Veteran	Summon Orc	R2	2/2	Cannot be assigned to block any creature of power greater than 1. R: First strike until end of turn.
Order of Leitbur	Summon Clerics	WW	2/1	Protection from black. W: First strike. WW: +1/+0 until end of turn.
Order of the Ebon Hand	Summon Clerics	BB	2/1	B: First strike BB: +1/+0 to end of turn.

Card	Type	Cost	P/T	Description
Order of the Sacred Torch	Summon Paladin	WW1	2/2	Tap and pay 1 life to counter target black spell. Effects that prevent or redirect damage done in ths way cannot be used to counter this loss of life. Use as an interrupt.
Order of the White Shield	Summon Knights	WW	2/1	Protection from black. W: First strike until end of turn. WW: +1/+0 until end of turn.
Orgg	Summon Orgg	RR3	6/6	Trample. Orgg may not attack if opponent controls an untapped creature of power greater than 2. Orgg cannot block any creature of power greater than 2.
Ornithopter	Artifact Creature	0	0/2	Flying.
Osai Vultures	Summon Vultures	W1	1/1	Flying. Gains a counter at end of turn if a creature went to the graveyard that turn. May turn in 2 counters for +1/+1 until end of turn.
Pale Bears	Summon Bears	G2	2/2	Islandwalk.
Palladia-Mors	Summon Elder Dragon Legend	GGRR WW2	7/7	Flying. Trample. Pay GRW during upkeep or card is buried.
Panic	Instant	R	--	Target creature cannot block this turn. Draw a card at the beginning of the next turn's upkeep.
Paralyze	Enchant Creature	B	--	Taps target creature when cast. Creature does not untap as normal, controller must pay 4 during upkeep to untap.
Pearled Unicorn	Summon Unicorn	W2	2/2	
Pentagram of the Ages	Artifact	4	--	Tap+(4) Prevent all damage dealt to you from one source. Does not prevent same source from damaging you again this round.
Personal Incarnation	Summon Avatar	WWW3	6/6	Can redirect damage from it to controller. Controller loses 1/2 of his life if it dies.
Pestilence	Enchantment	BB2	--	B: Does 1 damage to all creatures and all players. Removed from play if there are no creatures in play at end of turn.
Pestilence Rats	Summon Rats	B2	*/3	Where * is number of other rats in play.

Card	Type	Cost	P/T	Description
Petra Sphinx	Summon Sphinx	WWW2	3/4	Tap to have a player guess the top card of their library. If right he gets the card, if wrong it goes to the graveyard.
Phantasmal Forces	Summon Phantasm	U3	4/1	Flying. Pay U during your upkeep or Phantasmal Forces is destroyed.
Phantasmal Mount	Summon Phantasm	U1	1/1	Flying. Tap to give target creature with toughness less than 3 flying and +1/+1 until end of turn. Toughness may subsequently be increased. If either Mount or target leave play, other is buried.
Phantasmal Terrain	Enchant Land	UU	--	Target land becomes a basic land of caster's choice.
Phantom Monster	Summon Phantasm	U3	3/3	Flying.
Piety	Instant	W2	--	+0/+3 to all defending creatures until end of turn.
Pikemen	Summon Pikemen	W1	1/1	Banding. First strike.
Pirate Ship	Summon Ship	U4	4/3	Tap to do 1 damage to target. Opponent must have islands to attack with this card. Destroyed if you have no islands.
Pit Scorpion	Summon Scorpion	B2	1/1	Give opponent a poison counter each time it hits opponent. If opponent ever has 10 or more poison counters, he loses.
Pit Trap	Artifact	2	--	Tap+(2) Sacrifice to bury non-flying target creature that is attacking you this turn.
Plague Rats	Summon Rats	B2	*/*	Where * is number of Plague Rats in play.
Plains	Land	--	--	Tap to add W to your mana pool.
Polar Kraken	Summon Kraken	UUU8	11/11	Cumulative upkeep: Sacrifice a land. Trample. Comes into play tapped.
Portent	Sorcery	U	--	Look at top three cards of target player's library then shuffle it or return the three in any order. Draw a card at beginning of next turn's upkeep.
Power Leak	Enchant Enchantment	U1	--	Target's controller must pay 2 during their upkeep or take 1 damage for each unpaid mana.

Card	Type	Cost	P/T	Description
Power Sink	Interrupt	UX	--	Target spell is countered unless caster spends an additional X mana. If he or she cannot spend this mana all his or her lands are tapped.
Power Surge	Enchantment	RR	--	During upkeep phase, all players take 1 damage per land which was untapped at the beginning of turn.
Pox	Sorcery	BBB	--	Sacrifice, rounding up, 1/3 of life, hand, creatures, and lands in that order. Damage cannot be prevented.
Pradesh Gypsies	Summon Gypsies	G2	1/1	Tap+(G1) Give a creature -2/-0 until end of turn.
Primal Clay	Artifact Creature	4	*/*	When brought into play caster must select if it is a 1/6 wall, a 3/3 walker, or a 2/2 flyer.
Primordial Ooze	Summon Ooze	R	1/1	Must attack if possible. Get +1/+1 token each upkeep. Must pay 1 mana per token or it taps and you take damage equal to number of tokens.
Primal Order	Enchantment	GG2	--	During upkeep, Primal Order deals 1 damage to that player for each non-basic land he controls.
Prismatic Ward	Enchant Creature	W1	--	When it comes into play choose a color. Damage done to target creature by that color is reduced to 0.
Prodigal Sorcerer	Summon Wizard	U2	1/1	Tap to do 1 damage to any target.
Primal Order	Enchantment	GG2	--	During each player's upkeep, Primal Order deals one damage for each non-basic land they control.
Prophecy	Socery	W	--	Opponent reveals top card of his library. If a land, gain one life. He then reshuffles library. Controller draws one card at beginning of next upkeep.
Psionic Entity	Summon Entity	U4	2/2	Tap to do 2 damage to any target, but also does 3 damage to itself.
Psychic Venom	Enchant Land	U1	--	Whenever target land becomes tapped the land's controller suffers 2 points of damage.
Puppet Master	Enchant Creature	UUU	--	If target creature goes to the graveyard you may instead return it to your hand. If you pay UUU you may also return Puppet Master to your hand as well.

Card	Type	Cost	P/T	Description
Purelace	Interrupt	W	--	Changes color of target permanent to white.
Pygmy Allosaurus	Summon Dinosaur	G2	2/2	Swampwalk.
Pyknite	Summon Pyknite	G2	1/1	Draw a card at the beginning of the next turn's upkeep after summoning.
Pyroblast	Interrupt	R	--	Counter target spell if it is blue or destroy permanent if it is blue.
Pyroclasm	Sorcery	R1	--	Does 2 damage to each creature.
Pyrotechnics	Sorcery	R4	--	Distribute 4 damage among any targets.
Rabid Wombat	Summon Wombat	GG2	0/1	Does not tap when attacking. Gets +2/+2 for each enchantment on it.
Rack, The	Artifact	1	--	Opponent takes 1 damage for each card less than 3 in his or her hand.
Radjan Spirit	Summon Spirit	G3	3/2	Tap to remove flying from target creature until end of turn.
Rag Man	Summon Rag Man	BB2	2/1	Tap+(BBB) Look at opponent's hand; if it contains creatures he must discard one of them at random. This ability may only be used during its controller's turn.
Raiding Party	Enchantment	RR	--	Raiding Party may not be the target of white spells or effects. 0: Sacrifice an Orc to destroy all plains, a player may tap a white creature to prevent up to 2 plains from being destroyed. Any number of creatures may be tapped in this manner.
Rainbow Vale	Land	--	--	Tap to add 1 mana of any color to your mana pool, but control of Rainbow Vale then passes to opponent.
Raise Dead	Sorcery	B	--	Return target creature from graveyard to your hand.
Rakalite	Artifact	6	--	2: Prevent 1 damage to any target. Returns to hand on turn in which it is used.
Rally	Instant	WW	--	All blocking creatures in play get a +1/+1 bonus until end of turn.
Rashka the Slayer	Summon Legend	WW3	3/3	Can block creatures with flying. If assigned to block any black creature, Rashka gets +1/+2 until end of turn.

Card	Type	Cost	P/T	Description
Ray of Command	Instant	U3	--	Untap target creature opponent controls and gain control of it until end of turn. That creature can tap this turn. When you lose control of creature it becomes tapped.
Ray of Erasure	Instant	U	--	Target player takes the top card of their library and puts it in graveyard. Draw a card at beginning of next turn's upkeep.
Reality Twist	Enchantment	UUU	--	Cumulative upkeep: UU1. Instead of normal, plains produce R, swamps produce G, mountains produce W, and forests produce B.
Rebirth	Sorcery	GGG3	--	Each player may be healed to 20 life. Any player so choosing antes an additional card from the top of his library. Remove if not playing for ante.
Recall	Sorcery	UXX	--	Sacrifice X cards from your hand and bring X cards from your graveyard to your hand.
Reclamation	Enchantment	WG2	--	No black creature can attack unless its controller sacrifices a land.
Red Elemental Blast	Interrupt	R	--	Destroys a red card in play or counters a red spell as it is being cast.
Red Mana Battery	Artifact	4	--	Tap+(2) Add a token to Battery or tap to add R to your mana pool. Can convert counters to R.
Red Scarab	Enchant Creature	W	--	Target creature gets +2/+2 as long as opponent has red cards in play and cannot be blocked by red creatures.
Red Ward	Enchant Creature	W	--	Target creature gains protection from red.
Reef Pirates	Summon Ships	UU1	2/2	Whenever Reef Pirates damages any opponent take the top card of his or her library and place it in the graveyard.
Regeneration	Enchant Creature	G1	--	Target creature gains G: Regenerates.
Relic Bind	Enchant Artifact	U2	--	Give 1 life or 1 damage to a player whenever target artifact is tapped. Must be cast on opponent's artifact.
Remove Soul	Interrupt	U1	--	Counters target summon spell as it is being cast.

Card	Type	Cost	P/T	Description
Renewal	Sorcery	G2	--	Search through your library for a basic land and put it into play. This does not count towards the one land you can lay a turn. When this is done you must sacrifice a land. Draw a card during your next upkeep.
Repentant Blacksmith	Summon Smith	W1	1/2	Protection from red.
Retribution	Sorcery	RR2	--	Choose two target creatures controlled by an opponent. Bury one of those creatures, and put a -1/-1 counter on the other. That opponent chooses which creature is buried.
Reveka, Wizard Savant	Summon Legend	UU2	0/1	Tap: Reveka deals 2 damage to target creature or player and does not untap during your next untap phase.
Revelation	Enchant World	G	--	All players play with hand face up on the table.
Reverse Damage	Instant	WW1	--	All damage done to you from one source is instead added to your life.
Righteousness	Instant	W	--	Target defending creature gains +7/+7.
Rime Dryad	Summon Dryad	G	1/2	Snow-covered forestwalk.
Ring of Renewal	Artifact	5	--	Tap+(5) Discard a card at random from your hand and draw 2 cards.
Ritual of Subdual	Enchantment	GG4	--	Cumulative upkeep: 2. All lands produce colorless mana.
River Delta	Land	--	--	Does not untap if it has a depletion counter on it. During upkeep remove 1 depletion counter. Tap to add U or B to your mana pool and put one depletion counter on it.
River Merfolk	Summon Merfolk	UU	2/1	U: Mountainwalk until end of turn.
Rod of Ruin	Artifact	4	--	Tap+(3) Do 1 damage to any target.
Root Spider	Summon Spider	G3	2/2	If assigned as a blocker, Root Spider gains first strike and gets +1/+0 until end of turn.
Roots	Enchant Creature	G3	--	Tap target creature without flying. That creature does not untap during its controller's next untap phase.

Card	Type	Cost	P/T	Description
Roterothopter	Artifact Creature	1	0/2	Flying. 2: +1/+0 until the end of the turn. You cannot spend more more than four in this way each turn.
Royal Assassin	Summon Assassin	BB1	1/1	Tap to destroy 1 tapped creature.
Rubinia Soulsinger	Summon Legend	UGW2	2/3	Tap to control a creature; may choose not to untap. Lose control of creature if Rubinia leaves play or becomes untapped.
Ruins of Trokair	Land	--	--	Comes into play tapped. Tap to add W to your mana pool. Tap and sacrifice to add WW to your mana pool.
Runed Arch	Artifact	3	--	Comes into play tapped. Tap+(X) Sacrifice Runed Arch. X target creatures with power no greater than 2 cannot be blocked this turn. Later effect may increase target's powers.
Runesword	Artifact	6	--	Tap+(3) Attacking creature gains +2/+0 until end of turn. Any creature damaged by target creature may not regenerate. If a creature is placed in graveyard this turn it is removed from the game. If target creature leaves play this turn then Runesword is buried.
Rysorian Badger	Summon Badger	G2	2/2	If Rysorian Badger attacks and is not blocked, you may choose to have it deal no damage to defending player this turn. If you do so, remove from the game up to two target creatures from opponent's graveyard and gain one life for each creature removed in this way.
Sabretooth Tiger	Summon Tiger	R2	2/1	First strike.
Sacred Boon	Instant	W1	--	Prevent up to 3 damage to target creature in play. At end of turn, put a +0/+1 bonus counter on that creature for each 1 damage prevented in this way.
Safe Haven	Land	--	--	Tap+(2) to remove 1 creature you control from the game. This ability may be played as an interrupt. During upkeep sacrifice to return all creatures removed from the game by Safe Haven to game. Treat these creatures as if they were just summoned.

Card	Type	Cost	P/T	Description
Samite Alchemist	Summon Alchemist	W3	0/2	WW, Tap: Prevent up to four damage to a creature you control. Tap that creature. That creature does not untap during your next untap phase.
Samite Healer	Summon Cleric	W1	1/1	Tap to prevent one point of damage to any target.
Sand Silos	Land	--	--	Comes into play tapped. You may choose not to untap to add a storage counter. Tap and remove X storage counters to add X U to your mana pool.
Sandstorm	Instant	G	--	All attacking creatures take 1 damage.
Savannah Lions	Summon Lions	W	2/1	
Scaled Wurm	Summon Wurm	G7	7/6	
Scathe Zombies	Summon Zombies	B2	2/2	
Scavenger Folk	Summon Scavenger Folk	G	1/1	Tap+(G) Sacrifice Scavenger Folk to destroy target artifact.
Scavenging Ghoul	Summon Ghoul	B3	2/2	Add 1 token to Ghoul at end of turn for each creature that died during the turn. Remove 1 token to regenerate Ghoul.
Scryb Sprites	Summon Faeries	G	1/1	Flying.
Sea Serpent	Summon Serpent	U5	5/5	May not attack unless opponent controls at least one island. Destroyed if at any time you have no islands in play.
Sea Spirit	Summon Spirit	U4	2/3	U: +1/+0 until end of turn.
Sea Sprite	Summon Faerie	U1	1/1	Protection from red. Flying.
Sea Troll	Summon Troll	U2	2/1	U: Regenerate. Use ability only during a turn in which Sea Troll blocked a blue creature or blue creature blocked it.
Seasinger	Summon Merfolk	UU	10/1	Bury Seasinger if you have no islands in play. Tap to gain control of target creature if its controller controls at least 1 island. Lose control of target creature if Seasinger leaves play, if you lose control of Seasinger, or if it becomes untapped. You may choose not to untap as normal during your untap phase.

Card	Type	Cost	P/T	Description
Seeker	Enchant Creature	WW2	--	Target creature may only be blocked by white and artifact creatures.
Segovian Leviathan	Summon Leviathan	U4	3/3	Islandwalk.
Seizures	Enchant Creature	B1	--	When target creature becomes tapped, its controller suffers 3 points of damage. This can be prevented by paying 3.
Sengir Autocrat	Summon Autocrat	B3	2/2	When Autocrat enters play, place three Serf tokens into play. Treat tokens as 0/1 black creatures. If Autocrat leaves play bury all Serf tokens.
Sengir Bats	Summon Bats	BB1	1/2	Flying. Whenever a creature is put into the graveyard the same turn that the Sengir bats damaged it put a +1/+1 counter on the bat.
Sengir Vampire	Summon Vampire	BB3	4/4	Flying. Gets a +1/+1 token whenever a creature dies in a turn in which Sengir Vampire damaged it.
Sentinel	Artifact Creature	4	1/*	Where * is 1 at the time of casting but can be changed to X+1 during combat. X is the power of a creature blocking or blocked by Sentinel.
Seraph	Summon Angel	W6	4/4	Flying. Any creature which goes to the graveyard on a turn when damaged by Seraph is put directly into play under Seraph's controller's control at end of turn.
Serpent Generator	Artifact	6	--	Tap+(4) Create a 1/1 poisoned snake token creature. If snake damages opponent give opponent poison counter. If opponent has 10 or more poison counters he or she loses.
Serra Angel	Summon Angel	WW3	4/4	Flying. Does not tap when attacking.
Serra Aviary	Enchant World	W3	--	All creatures with flying get +1/+1.
Serra Bestiary	Enchant Creature	WW	--	During upkeep pay two white or bury Bestiary. Target creature cannot attack, block, or use ability that includes tap in the activation cost.

Card	Type	Cost	P/T	Description
Serra Inquisitors	Summon Inquisitors	W4	3/3	Serra Inquisitors gets +2/+0 until the end of turn if assigned to block or is blocked by any black creatures.
Serra Paladin	Summon Paladin	WW2	2/2	Tap to prevent one damage to any creature or player. 1WW, Tap: Attacking does not cause target creature to tap.
Serrated Arrows	Artifact	4	--	When Serrated Arrows come into play put three arrowhead counters on it. Tap to place a -1/-1 arrowhead counter on target creature. When Arrows have no more counters on them bury Arrows at the end of the turn.
Shambling Strider	Summon Strider	GG4	5/5	GR: +1/-1 until end of turn.
Shanodin Dryads	Summon Nymphs	G	1/1	Forestwalk.
Shapeshifter	Artifact Creature	6	*/7-*	Where * is chosen on casting and during each of controller's upkeeps. * can be any number 1-6.
Shatter	Instant	R1	--	Destroys target artifact.
Shield Bearer	Summon Soldier	W1	0/3	Banding.
Shield of the Ages	Artifact	2	--	2: Prevent 1 damage to you.
Shield Wall	Instant	W1	--	+0/+2 to all your creatures until end of turn.
Shimian Nightstalker	Summon Nightstalker	BB3	4/4	Tap+(B) Redirect damage done to you by one creature to Nightstalker.
Shivan Dragon	Summon Dragon	RR4	5/5	Flying. R: +1/+0 until end of turn.
Shrink	Instant	G	--	Target creature gets -5/-0 until the end of turn.
Shyft	Summon Shyft	U4	4/2	During your upkeep may change it to any color or combination of colors.
Sibilant Spirit	Summon Spirit	U5	5/6	Flying. Whenever declared as an attacker, defender may draw a card.
Silver Erne	Summon Erne	U3	2/2	Flying, trample.
Simulacrum	Instant	B1	--	Transfer all damage done to you so far this turn to a creature.
Sinbad	Summon Sinbad	U1	1/1	Tap to draw 1 card. Discard this card unless it is a land.

Card	Type	Cost	P/T	Description
Siren's Call	Instant	U	--	All of opponent's non-wall creatures must attack. If a creature is unable to attack, it is destroyed.
Sisters of the Flame	Summon Sisters	RR1	2/2	Tap to add R to your mana pool. This ability may be used as an interrupt.
Sivitri Scarzam	Summon Legend	BU5	6/4	
Skeleton Ship	Summon Legend	UB3	0/3	If at any time the caster controls no islands this card must be burried. Tap to put -1/-1 counter on target creature.
Skull Catapult	Artifact	4	--	Tap+(1) Sacrifice a creature to have Skull Catapult deal 2 damage to a target.
Sleight of Mind	Interrupt	U	--	Changes color reference on a spell or permanent.
Smoke	Enchantment	RR	--	Players may only untap 1 creature during untap phase.
Snow-Covered Forest	Land	--	--	Tap to add G to your mana pool.
Snow-Covered Island	Land	--	--	Tap to add U to your mana pool.
Snow-Covered Mountain	Land	--	--	Tap to add R to your mana pool.
Snow-Covered Plains	Land	--	--	Tap to add W to your mana pool.
Snow-Covered Swamp	Land	--	--	Tap to add B to your mana pool.
Snow Devil	Enchant Creature	U1	--	Target creature gains flying. As long as you control any snow-covered lands also gains first strike when blocking.
Snow Fortress	Artifact Creature	5	0/4	Counts as a wall. 1: +1/+0 to Snow Fortress' power until end of turn. 1: +0/+1 to Snow Fortress' toughness until end of turn. 3: Deal 1 damage to target creature without flying that is attacking you.
Snow Hound	Summon Dog	W2	1/1	Tap+(1): Return Snow Hound to owner's hand from play and target blue or green creature in play you control to owner's hand.

Card	Type	Cost	P/T	Description
Snowblind	Enchant Creature	G3	--	Target creature gets -*/-*. When attacking * = number of snow-covered lands defender controls. All other times * = number of snow-covered lands controller controls.
Snowfall	Enchantment	U2	--	Cumulative upkeep: U. Islands may produce an additional U when tapped for mana which is usable only for cumulative upkeep. Snow-covered islands may produce an additional UU or U which is only usable for cumulative upkeep.
Sol 'kanar the Swamp King	Summon Legend	BUR2	5/5	Swampwalk. Gain 1 life each time a black spell is cast.
Soldevi Golem	Artifact Creature	4	5/3	Soldevi Golem does not untap during your untap phase. 0: Untap target creature opponent controls to untap Soldevi Golem at the end of your upkeep. Use this ability only during your upkeep.
Soldevi Machinist	Summon Wizard	U1	1/1	Tap to add 2 to your mana pool which can only be used for activation costs of an artifact. Use this ability as an interrupt.
Soldevi Simulacrum	Artifact Creature	4	2/4	Cumulative upkeep: 1. 1: +1/+0 to Soldevi Simulacrum's power until end of turn.
Songs of the Damned	Interrupt	B	--	Add B to your mana pool for each creature in your graveyard.
Soraya the Falconer	Summon Legend	WW1	2/2	All Falcons get +1/+1. W1: Target Falcon gains banding until end of turn.
Sorceress Queen	Summon Sorceress	BB1	1/1	Tap to make a creature 0/2 until end of turn.
Soul Barrier	Enchantment	U2	--	Whenever target opponent casts a summon spell, deals 2 damage to him. He may pay 2 to prevent this.
Soul Burn	Sorcery	B2	--	Does 1 damage to target for each B or R spent in addition to cost. You gain 1 life for each damage you inflict this way.

Card	Type	Cost	P/T	Description
Soul Exchange	Sorcery	BB	--	Sacrifice a creature, but remove it from the game instead of putting it in the graveyard. Remove 1 creature from the graveyard and put it directly into play as if it were just summoned. If sacrificed creature was a Thrull put a +2/+2 on creature.
Soul Kiss	Enchant Creature	B2	--	B: Pay 1 life point and target creature enchanted by Soul Kiss gains +2/+2 until end of turn. You may not spend more than BBB each turn. Effects that redirect or prevent damage cannot be used to counter this.
Soul Net	Artifact	1	--	1: Gain 1 life whenever a creature goes to the graveyard.
Spectral Bears	Summon Bears	G1	3/3	If Bears is declared as attacker and defending player controls no black cards, it will not untap duing your next untap phase.
Spectral Shield	Enchant Creature	WU1	--	Target creature in play gets a +0/+2 bonus to its toughness. That creature cannot be the target of any other spells after Spectral Shield enchants it.
Spell Blast	Interrupt	UX	--	Target spell of casting cost X is countered.
Spirit Link	Enchant Creature	W	--	For each point of damage target creature does controller gains 1 life.
Spirit Shackle	Enchant Creature	BB	--	Target gets a -0/-2 counter each time it is tapped.
Spirit Shield	Artifact	3	--	Tap+(2) Target creature gets +0/+2 as long as Spirit Shield remains tapped. You may choose not to untap Shield as normal during your untap phase.
Spoils of Evil	Interrupt	B2	--	Add 1 colorless mana to your pool and gain 1 life for each artifact or creature in opponent's graveyard.
Spoils of War	Sorcery	BX	--	Put X +1/+1 bonus counters on any number of target creatures in play. X is the number of creatures and artifacts in opponent's graveyard.

Card	Type	Cost	P/T	Description
Spore Cloud	Instant	GG1	--	Tap all blocking creatures. No creatures deal damage in combat this turn. Neither attacking nor blocking creatures untap as normal during their controller's next untap phase.
Spore Flower	Summon Fungus	GG	0/1	During your upkeep, put a spore counter on Spore Flower. 0: Remove 3 spore counters from Spore Flower. No creatures deal damage in combat this turn.
Staff of the Ages	Artifact	3	--	Creatures with any landwalking ability may be blocked as if they did not have any landwalking abilities.
Stampede	Instant	GG1	--	All attacking creatures get trample and +1/+0 until end of turn.
Stangg	Summon Legend	GR4	3/4	When Stangg comes into play also place a 3/4 red and green Stangg Twin token into play. If either Stangg or Twin leaves play the other does as well.
Stasis	Enchantment	U1	--	All players skip their untap phase. Controller must pay U during upkeep or Stasis is destroyed.
Steal Artifact	Enchant Artifact	UU2	--	Target artifact comes under caster's control.
Stench of Evil	Sorcery	BB2	--	Destroy all plains. Does 1 damage for each plains destroyed this way to controller. Damage may be prevented for 2 each points.
Stone Giant	Summon Giant	RR2	3/4	Tap to make a creature of toughness less than Giant's power flying until end of turn. Target creature is destroyed at end of turn.
Stone Rain	Sorcery	R2	--	Destroy any 1 land in play.
Stone Spirit	Summon Spirit	R4	4/3	Creatures with flying may not block Stone Spirit.
Stonehands	Enchant Creature	R2	--	Target creature gains +0/+2. R: +1/+0 until end of turn.
Storm Seeker	Instant	G3	--	Opponent takes on damage for each card in their hand.
Storm Spirit	Summon Spirit	WUG3	3/3	Flying. Tap to deal 2 damage to target creature.

Card	Type	Cost	P/T	Description
Stormbind	Enchantment	RG1	--	2: Discard a card at random from your hand to deal 2 damage to target creature or player.
Stream of Life	Sorcery	GX	--	Target player gains X life.
Strip Mine	Land	--	--	Tap to add 1 colorless mana to your pool. Tap and sacrifice to destroy any one land.
Stromgald Cabal	Summon Knights	BB1	2/2	Tap and pay 1 life to counter target white spell. Damage cannot be prevented. Play as an interrupt.
Stunted Growth	Sorcery	GG3	--	Target player takes 3 cards from hand and puts them on top of library in any order.
Sulfurous Springs	Land	--	--	Tap to add 1 to your mana pool or tap to add B or R to your mana pool and does 1 damage to you.
Sunglasses of Urza	Artifact	3	--	Allows white mana to be used as red mana.
Sunken City	Enchantment	UU	--	Adds +1/+1 to all blue creatures in play. Controller must pay UU during upkeep or Sunken City is buried.
Sunstone	Artifact	3	--	2: Sacrifice a snow-covered land in play to have all creatures in play deal no damage during combat this turn.
Svyelunite Priest	Summon Merfolk	U1	1/1	Tap+(UU) Target creature may not be the target of spells or fast effects until end of turn. Use this ability only during your upkeep.
Svyelunite Temple	Land	--	--	Comes into play tapped. Tap to add U to your mana pool. Sacrifice and tap to add UU to your mana pool.
Swamp	Land	--	--	Tap to add B to your mana pool.
Swords to Plowshares	Instant	W	--	Remove target creature from the game. Creature's controller gains life equal to target's power.
Sylvan Library	Enchantment	G1	--	May draw 2 extra cards during draw then put 2 back on the library in any order. Lose 4 life for each card not put back.

Card	Type	Cost	P/T	Description
Takklemaggot	Enchant Creature	BB2	--	Target gets -0/-1 counter during each upkeep. When target goes to the graveyard, its controller picks another creature to place Takklemaggot on. If there are no creatures in play it becomes an enchantment and does 1 damage each turn to controller of last creature to die.
Tarpan	Summon Tarpan	G	1/1	If goes to graveyard from play gain 1 life.
Tawnos's Wand	Artifact	4	--	Tap+(2) Makes a creature of power less than 2 blockable only by artifact creatures until end of turn.
Tawnos's Weaponry	Artifact	2	--	Tap+(2) Add +1/+1 to target creature. Effect remains until untapped. May choose not to untap.
Teleport	Instant	UUU	--	Makes a creature unblockable until end of turn. Play after attackers are chosen but before blockers are chosen.
Tempest Efreet	Summon Efreet	RRR1	3/3	Tap and bury Efreet in opponent's graveyard to take a random card from his hand into yours. Swap is permanent. Can be countered by losing 10 life. Play only in ante games.
Terror	Instant	B1	--	Target creature is buried.
Tetravus	Artifact Creature	6	1/1	Flying. Starts with 3 +1/+1 tokens on it. During upkeep can convert tokens to or from 1/1 flying artifact creatures which cannot be enchanted.
Thallid	Summon Fungus	G	1/1	During your upkeep, put a spore counter on Thallid. 0: Remove 3 spore counters from Thallid to put a Saporling token into play. Treat this token as a 1/1 green creature.
Thallid Devourer	Summon Fungus	GG1	2/2	During your upkeep, put a spore counter on Thallid Devourer. 0: Remove 3 spore counters from Thallid Devourer to put a Saporling token into play. Treat this token as a 1/1 green creature. 0: Sacrifice a Saporling to give Thallid Devourer +1/+2 until end of turn.

Card	Type	Cost	P/T	Description
Thelon's Chant	Enchantment	GG1	--	During your upkeep pay G or bury Thelon's Chant. Whenever a player puts a swamp into play Thelon's Chant does 3 damage to him unless he puts a -1/-1 counter onto a creature that he controls.
Thelon's Curse	Enchantment	GG	--	Blue creatures do not untap as normal during their controller's upkeep. During their upkeep controller of these blue creatures may spend an additional U to untap one creature. Each creature may only be untapped in this fashion once.
Thelonite Druid	Summon Cleric	G2	1/1	Tap+(G1) Sacrifice a creature to turn all your forests into 2/3 creatures until end of turn. The forests still count as lands but may not be tapped for mana if they were brought into play this turn.
Thelonite Monk	Summon Cleric	GG2	1/2	Tap to sacrifice a green creature to turn a target land into a basic forest. Mark changed land with a counter.
Thermokarst	Sorcery	GG1	--	Destroy target land. If it is snow-covered gain 1 life.
Thicket Basilisk	Summon Basilisk	GG3	2/4	All non-wall creatures blocking or blocked by Basilisk are destroyed at the end of combat.
Thorn Thallid	Summon Fungus	GG1	2/2	During your upkeep, put a spore counter on Thorn Thallid. 0: Remove 3 spore counters from Thorn Thallid to do 1 damage to any target.
Thoughtlace	Interrupt	U	--	Changes color of one card to blue.
Thoughtleech	Enchantment	GG	--	Whenever opponent taps an island gain 1 life.
Throne of Bone	Artifact	1	--	1: Gain 1 life whenever a black spell is cast.
Thrull Champion	Summon Thrull	B4	2/2	All Thrulls in play gain +1/+1. Tap to take control of target Thrull. You lose control of target Thrull if Champion leaves play or you lose control of Champion.
Thrull Retainer	Enchant Creature	B	--	Target gets +1/+1. Sacrifice Thrull Retainer to regenerate target.
Thrull Wizards	Summon Thrull	B2	1/1	Counters target black spell unless caster plays an additional B or 3.
Thunder Wall	Summon Wall	UU1	0/2	Flying. U: +1/+1 until end of turn.

Card	Type	Cost	P/T	Description
Tidal Flats	Enchantment	U	--	UU: All your blocking creatures that are blocking non-flying creatures gain first strike until end of turn. The attacking player may pay 1 for each attacking creature to prevent Tidal Flats from giving that creature's blockers first strike.
Tidal Influence	Enchantment	U2	--	Put a tide counter on Tidal Influence when it is brought into play and during your upkeep. If there is 1 tide counter on Tidal Influence all blue creatures get -2/-0. If there are 3 counters on Tidal Influence all blue creatures get +2/+0. If there are 4 counters on Tidal Influence remove them all. You may not cast Tidal Influence if there is another Tidal Influence already in play.
Timber Wolves	Summon Wolves	G	1/1	Banding.
Timberline Ridge	Land	--	--	Does not untap if it has depletion counter on it. Remove 1 depletion counter during upkeep. Tap to add R or G to your mana pool and put 1 depletion counter on it.
Time Bomb	Artifact	4	--	During your upkeep, gains a time counter. Tap+(1) Sacrifice to deal X damage to each creature and player where X is the number of time counters on it.
Time Elemental	Summon Elemental	U2	0/2	Tap+(UU2) Send target permanent to owner's hand. Take 5 damage and destroy Elemental if is used to attack or block.
Timmerian Fiends	Summon Fiends	BB1	1/1	BBB: Sacrifice Fiends into opponent's graveyard to bury target artifact that opponent owns into your graveyard.
Tinder Wall	Summon Wall	G	0/3	0: Sacrifice to add RR to your pool. R: Sacrifice to deal 2 damage to target creature it blocks.
Titania's Song	Enchantment	G3	--	All artifacts in play become artifact creatures with power and toughness equal to their casting cost. They do not retain their abilities as artifacts.
Tobias Andrion	Summon Legend	UW3	4/4	

Card	Type	Cost	P/T	Description
Tor Giant	Summon Giant	R3	3/3	
Tor Wauki	Summon Legend	BBR2	3/3	Tap to do 2 damage to an attacking or blocking creature.
Tormod's Crypt	Artifact	0	--	Tap and sacrifice to remove all cards in target player's graveyard from the game.
Torture	Enchant Creature	B	--	Choose target creature. B1: Put a -1/-1 counter on creature Tourture enchants.
Total War	Enchantment	R3	--	When a player declares an attack, all their creatures must attack or die, except walls and creatures not controlled at beginning of turn.
Touch of Death	Sorcery	B2	--	Deals 1 damage to target player and you gain 1 life. Draw a card at the beginning of the next turn's upkeep.
Touch of Vitae	Instant	G2	--	Untap target creature. Draw a card at the beginning of the next turn's upkeep.
Tourach's Chant	Enchantment	BB1	--	During your upkeep, pay B or destroy Tourach's Chant. Whenever a player puts a forest into play, does 3 damage to him, unless he puts a -1/-1 creature on a creature he controls.
Tourach's Gate	Enchant Land	BB1	--	Can only be played on a target land you control. Sacrifice a Thrull to place 3 time counters. During your upkeep remove a time counter and bury when none remain. 0: Tap land Gate enchants to give attacking creatures +2/-1 to end of turn.
Trade Caravan	Summon Caravan	W	1/1	During your upkeep, put a currency counter on Trade Caravan. 0: Remove two curency counters during opponent's upkeep and untap target land.
Trailblazer	Instant	GG2	--	Target creature cannot be blocked this turn.
Tranquility	Sorcery	G2	--	Destroys all enchantments in play.
Transmutation	Instant	B1	--	Switch power and toughness of creature until end of turn. Effects that alter power and toughness are also switched.
Triassic Egg	Artifact	4	--	Tap+(3) Put one counter on Egg. Sacrifice Egg with 2 or more counters and bring any creature from your hand or graveyard directly into play.

Card	Type	Cost	P/T	Description
Triskelion	Artifact Creature	6	1/1	Begins with 3 +1/+1 counters. May remove a counter at any time to do 1 damage to any target.
Truce	Instant	W2	--	Each player may draw up to two cards. For each card less than two any player draws, that player gains two life.
Tsunami	Sorcery	G3	--	Destroys all islands in play.
Tundra Wolves	Summon Wolves	W	1/1	First strike.
Twiddle	Instant	U	--	Tap or untap 1 creature, land, or artifact.
Uncle Istvan	Summon Uncle Istvan	BBB1	1/3	All damage done to Uncle Istvan by creatures is reduced to 0.
Underground River	Land	--	--	Tap to add 1 to your mana pool or tap to add U or B to your mana pool and does 1 damage to you.
Unholy Strength	Enchant Creature	B	--	Target gains +2/+1.
Unstable Mutation	Enchant Creature	U	--	Target creature gains +3/+3. During controller's upkeep put a -1/-1 counter on target. Tokens remain even if enchantment is removed.
Unsummon	Instant	U	--	Return target creature to controller's hand.
Untamed Wilds	Sorcery	G2	--	Bring one basic land from library into play.
Updraft	Instant	U1	--	Target creature gains flying until end of turn. Draw a card from the library at beginning of next turn's upkeep phase.
Urza's Avenger	Artifact Creature	6	4/4	Each upkeep give bands flying, trample, and or first strike at -1/-1 for each.
Urza's Bauble	Artifact	0	--	Tap and sacrifice Urza's Bauble to choose a card at random from target player's hand and look at it. Draw a card at the beginning of the next turn's upkeep.
Urza's Mine	Land	--	--	Tap to add 1 colorless mana to your pool. If you also control Urza's Powerplant and Urza's Tower, tap to add 2 colorless mana to your pool.

Card	Type	Cost	P/T	Description
Urza's Powerplant	Land	--	--	Tap to add 1 colorless mana to your pool. If you also control Urza's Mine and Urza's Tower, tap to add 2 colorless mana to your pool.
Urza's Tower	Land	--	--	Tap to add 1 colorless mana to your pool. If you also control Urza's Mine and Urza's Power Plant, tap to add 3 colorless mana to your pool.
Uthden Troll	Summon Troll	R2	2/2	R: Regenerates.
Vaevictis Asmadi	Summon Elder Dragon Legend	BBGG RR2	7/7	Flying. (B or G or R): +1/+0. Pay BGR during upkeep or this card is buried.
Vampire Bats	Summon Bats	B	0/1	B: +1/+0 until end of turn. Only BB may be spent in this fashion.
Veldrane of Sengir	Summon Legend	BB5	5/5	1BB: Forestwalk and -3/-0 until end of turn.
Veldt	Land	--	--	Does not untap if it has depletion counter on it. During upkeep remove 1 depletion counter. Tap to add W or G to your mana pool and place 1 depletion counter on it.
Venom	Enchant Creature	GG1	--	All non-wall creatures target creature blocks or is blocked by are destroyed at end of combat.
Venomous Breath	Instant	G3	--	At end of combat
Verduran Enchantress	Summon Enchantress	GG1	0/2	While Enchantress is in play, you may draw a card whenever you cast an enchantment.
Vertigo	Instant	R	--	Vertigo deals 2 damage to target creature with flying and it loses flying until end of turn.
Vexing Arcanix	Artifact	4	--	Tap+(3) Target player names a card and turns over top card of his library. If a named card it goes to player's hand, otherwise it goes to graveyard and Arcanix does 2 damage to target player.
Vibrating Sphere	Artifact	4	--	During your turn, all creatures you control get a +2/+0 bonus to their power and toughness. During all other turns, all creatures you control get -0/-2 to their power and toughness.
Visions	Sorcery	W	--	Look at top 5 cards of any library. Then you may choose to reshuffle it.

Card	Type	Cost	P/T	Description
Vodalian Knights	Summon Merfolk	UU1	2/2	First strike. U: Flying until end of turn. Vodalian Knights may not attack unless your opponent controls at least one island. Bury if you control no islands.
Vodalian Mage	Summon Merfolk	U2	1/1	Tap+(U) Counters target spell unless caster of spell spends an additional 1. Play this ability as an interrupt.
Vodalian Soldiers	Summon Merfolk	U1	1/2	
Vodalian War Machine	Summon Wall	UU1	0/4	0: Tap target Merfolk you control to allow Vodalian War Machine to attack this turn or give a +2/+1 until end of turn. If Vodalian War Machine is put in the graveyard, all Merfolk tapped in this manner this turn are destroyed.
Volcanic Eruption	Sorcery	UUUX	--	Destroys X mountains and does X damage to all creatures and players for each mountain destroyed.
Voodoo Doll	Artifact	6	--	Add one token each upkeep. Tap+(XX) Do X damage to any target. X is the number of tokens on Voodoo Doll. If Voodoo Doll ends the turn untapped you take X damage and Doll is destroyed.
Walking Wall	Artifact Creature	4	0/6	Counts as a wall. 3: Gets +3/-1 to walking wall's power and toughness until end of turn and can attack this turn. Cannot attack the turn it comes under your control and use this ability only once per turn.
Wall of Air	Summon Wall	UU1	1/5	Wall. Flying.
Wall of Bone	Summon Wall	B2	1/4	Wall. B: Regenerates.
Wall of Brambles	Summon Wall	G2	2/3	Wall. G: Regenerates
Wall of Dust	Summon Wall	R2	1/4	Wall. Creatures blocked by wall may not attack next turn.
Wall of Fire	Summon Wall	RR1	0/5	Wall. R: +1/+0 until end of turn.
Wall of Heat	Summon Wall	R2	2/6	Wall.
Wall of Ice	Summon Wall	G2	0/7	Wall.
Wall of Kelp	Summon Wall	UU	0/3	UU, Tap: Put a Kelp token into play; treat this token as a 0/1 blue wall.
Wall of Lava	Summon Wall	RR1	1/3	Wall. R: +1/+1 until end of turn.
Wall of Opposition	Summon Wall	RR3	0/6	1: +1/+0 until end of turn.

Card	Type	Cost	P/T	Description
Wall of Pine Needles	Summon Wall	G3	3/3	G: Regenerates.
Wall of Shadows	Summon Wall	BB1	0/1	Wall. Takes no damage when blocking creatures. Cannot be targeted by effects that target only walls.
Wall of Shields	Artifact Creature	3	0/4	Counts as a wall, banding.
Wall of Spears	Artifact Creature	3	2/3	Counts as wall. First strike.
Wall of Stone	Summon Wall	RR1	0/8	Wall.
Wall of Swords	Summon Wall	W3	3/5	Wall. Flying.
Wall of Vapor	Summon Wall	U3	0/1	Takes no damage when blocking creatures.
Wall of Water	Summon Wall	UU1	0/5	Wall. U: +1/+0
Wall of Wonder	Summon Wall	UU2	1/5	Wall. UU2: +4/-4 and can attack.
Wall of Wood	Summon Wall	G	0/3	Wall.
Wanderlust	Enchant Creature	G2	--	Does 1 damage to creature's controller during upkeep.
War Chariot	Artifact	3	--	Tap+(3) Target creature gains trample until end of turn.
War Elephant	Summon Elephant	W3	2/2	Trample. Bands.
War Mammoth	Summon Mammoth	G3	3/3	Trample.
Warning	Instant	W	--	Target attacking creature deals no damage in combat this round.
Warp Artifact	Enchant Artifact	BB	--	Does 1 damage to target's controller during his upkeep.
Water Elemental	Summon Elemental	UU3	5/4	
Weakness	Enchant Creature	B	--	Target gains -2/-1.
Web	Enchant Creature	G	--	Target creature gains +0/+2 and may block flying creatures.
Whalebone Glider	Artifact	2	--	Tap+(2) Target creature with power no greater than 3 gains flying until end of turn. Power may be increased afterwards.
Whirling Dervish	Summon Dervish	GG	1/1	Protection from black. Gets a +1/+1 token each time it damages opponent.

Card	Type	Cost	P/T	Description
White Knight	Summon Knight	WW	2/2	First strike. Protection from black.
White Mana Battery	Artifact	4	--	Tap+(2) Add 1 token to Battery. Tap to add W to your mana pool. Can convert tokens to W.
White Scarab	Enchant Creature	W	--	Target creature gets +2/+2 as long as opponent controls white cards and cannot be blocked by white creatures.
White Ward	Enchant Creature	W	--	Target creature gains protection from white.
Whiteout	Instant	G1	--	All creatures lose flying until end of turn.
Wiitigo	Summon Wiitigo	GGG3	0/0	When comes into play put 6 +1/+1 counters on it. During your upkeep if it has blocked or been blocked since last upkeep put a +1/+1 counter on it; otherwise remove a +1/+1 counter. Ignore this effect if there are no counters left.
Wild Growth	Enchant Land	G	--	Target land generates an additional G.
Will-O-The-Wisp	Summon Will-O-The-Wisp	B	0/1	Flying. B: Regenerates.
Willow Faerie	Summon Faerie	G1	1/2	Flying.
Willow Priestess	Summon Faerie	GG2	2/2	Tap: Place Faerie from your hand into play as though just summoned. G2: Target green creature gains protection from black until the end of the turn.
Wind Spirit	Summon Spirit	U4	3/2	Flying. Must be blocked by more than one creature during combat.
Winds of Change	Sorcery	R	--	Both players shuffle their hands into their library and draw up to the same number of cards as before.
Wings of Aesthir	Enchant Creature	WU	--	Target creature gains flying, first strike, and gets +1/+0.
Winter Blast	Sorcery	GX	--	Taps X creatures and does 2 damage to each of them that has flying ability.
Winter Orb	Artifact	2	--	Each player may only untap one land during untap phase.

Card	Type	Cost	P/T	Description
Winter Sky	Sorcery	R	--	Flip a coin; target opponent calls heads or tails while coin is in the air. If the flip is in his favor each player draws a card. If the flip is in your favor Winter Sky deals one damage to each creature and player.
Winter's Chill	Instant	UX	--	Cast only during combat before defense is chosen. At end of combat, destroy X attacking creatures in play. X cannot be greater than the number of snow-covered lands you control and have in play. For each attacking creature, opponent may pay 1 or 2 to prevent it from being destroyed. If 1, creature neither deals nor receives damage; if 2, deals and receives as normal.
Witch Hunter	Summon Hunter	WW2	1/1	Tap to do 1 damage to any player. Tap+(WW1) Return target creature to owner's hand. All enchantments on creatures are destroyed.
Withering Wisps	Enchantment	BB1	--	If at the end of the turn there are no creatures in play destroy Withering Wisps. B: Withering Wisps deals 1 point of damage to each creature and player. Its controller may not spend more B in this manner than his snow-covered swamps.
Wizard's School	Land	--	--	Tap to add one colorless mana to your mana pool. Tap and pay one colorless to add one U to your mana pool. Tap and pay two and add one W or one B to your mana pool.
Wooden Sphere	Artifact	1	--	1: Gain 1 life each time a green spell is cast.
Woolly Mammoths	Summon Mammoths	GG1	3/2	Gains trample as long as you have any snow-covered lands.
Woolly Spider	Summon Spider	GG1	2/3	Can block flying creatures. Gains +0/+2 if blocking a flying creature.
Word of Binding	Sorcery	BBX	--	X target creatures become tapped.
Word of Blasting	Instant	R1	--	Bury target wall. Does an amount of damage to controller equal to wall's casting cost.

Card	Type	Cost	P/T	Description
Word of Undoing	Instant	U	--	Target creature returns to owner's hand. Any white enchantments that you own on that creature return to your hand.
Wrath of God	Sorcery	WW2	--	All creatures in play are destroyed and may not regenerate.
Wrath of Marit Lage	Enchantment	UU3	--	When it comes into play tap all red creatures. Red creatures do not untap during their controller's untap phase.
Wretched, The	Summon Wretched	BB3	2/5	At end of turn take control of all creatures which block this card. Lose control of creatures if card leaves play or your control.
Xenic Poltergeist	Summon Poltergeist	BB1	1/1	Tap to turn an artifact into an artifact creature with power and toughness equal to its casting cost until the beginning of your next turn.
Xira Arien	Summon Legend	BGR	1/2	Flying. Tap+(BGR) Draw an extra card.
Yavimaya Gnats	Summon Insects	G2	0/1	Flying. G: Regenerate.
Yawgmoth Demon	Summon Demon	BB4	6/6	Flying. First strike. Sacrifice an artifact during upkeep or take 2 damage and Demon taps.
Yotian Soldier	Artifact Creature	3	1/4	Does not tap when attacking.
Zelyon Sword	Artifact	3	--	Tap+(3) Target creature gets +2/+0 as long as Zelyon Sword is tapped. You may choose not to untap.
Zephyr Falcon	Summon Falcon	U1	1/1	Flying. Does not tap when attacking.
Zombie Master	Summon Lord	BB1	2/3	All Zombies in play get swampwalk and regeneration.
Zur's Weirding	Enchantment	U3	--	All players play with cards in their hands face up. Whenever any player draws a card, any other player may pay 2 life to force the player to discard this card. Damage cannot be prevented.
Zuran Enchanter	Summon Wizard	U1	1/1	Tap+(2B): Target player chooses and discards one card from his hand. Ignore this ability if target has no cards. Use this ability only during your turn.

Card	Type	Cost	P/T	Description
Zuran Orb	Artifact	0	--	0: Sacrifice a land to gain 2 life.
Zuran Spellcaster	Summon Wizard	U2	1/1	Tap to deal one damage to target creature or player.

Index

Restricted, Type II cards, 132
Roads to victory, 6

S

Sammon, Brian, 72, 81-83
Small Creature decks, 3
Song and Surge, 73
Spy, The, 66-67
Stasis decks, 97-102
    cards that work well in, 97
Stasis Fireball Deck, The, 100-101
Stern, Henry, 58-59
Stern's Green / White Tome, 58
Surprise value, 7
Susa, Alvaro, 47

T

Tier theory of deck ranking, 21-22
Time Trap, The, 98-99
Titania's Book, 52-53
Tome decks, 49-59
Trade Caravan, The, 101-102

Turn economy, 4-5

U

Utility, measuring card economy,
    2-3

W

Weird Bottle, 84-85
Weird Hippy Shakes, The, 83-84
Weirding Stone, The, 65-66
Winter Fire in the Swamp, 92-93
Winter Orb decks, 89-95
*Wiseman and Pantages' (W&P)
    Book*, 54-55
Wiseman, Henry 54
White, fast mana, 14

Z

Zuran Orb, 29
Zur's Weirding decks, 81-87